# Claiming a Larger Gospel

## Overlooked Biblical Foundations
## for Those Aspiring to Grow in the Faith

by

# Cedric Holman Jaggard

*Foreword by David O. Moberg, Ph.D.*
*Developmental Editor: Rev. Joel E. Kok, Ph.D.*
*Copy Editors: Dennis and Rita Dern*
*Cover Design: Rita Dern*

# *Dedication*

## To Two Kindergarten Teachers

The first: My mother, Grace Perrine Holman Jaggard. She enjoyed a Christian heritage as the child of The Reverend and Mrs. Samuel A. Holman. Grace's desire to teach surfaced when she was in kindergarten. During her formative years, Grace was sent to a Quaker school in Philadelphia, followed by two years at Lasell Seminary for Young Women in Massachusetts. Her post-Lasell life reflected the breadth of outlook, Christian concern, and opportunities of her training, both in Christian and secular subjects. Widowed at 49, my mother chose to use income from her father's estate to graciously and generously provide my brother and me with education in the important secondary years. Grace Perrine Holman Jaggard lived to age 88.

The second: My wife, Jean Dale McGiffert Jaggard. Jean Dale had grown up as an only child in New Jersey. Her parents, Adele Post McGiffert and Crosby Jaquith McGiffert, loved her deeply.

After four years at Oberlin, America's first coed college, Jean Dale miraculously escaped - neither married nor engaged. She returned to her parents' home where she enjoyed a very successful first year of teaching kindergarten. The McGiffert family attended Grace Presbyterian Church. By God's grace, it was the fellowship I had turned to only a couple of years earlier following my return from European study with Karl Barth.

3

One Sunday night, after the meeting of the young adult group, which I had attended for a couple years, I noticed a new woman I had not seen before. After a mutual friend's introduction, our courtship began in June 1942 and the following year our marriage took place.

Jean Dale's love for children gave our two sons and our daughter a wonderful start in life. We were blessed that they married spouses whom are equally loved. Our family continues to grow with beautiful grandchildren and great-grandchildren.

Jean Dale took an active role in my pastorates. We eventually settled in Whitefish Bay, Wisconsin, a small village on Milwaukee's North Shore, where Jean Dale taught an additional 19 years of kindergarten.

Wherever possible along that trail, we "teamed together" – as Jean Dale so often expressed it – and each took a vital interest in the work of the other.

In time, including during the time spent writing this book, I realized how task oriented I had been and sought to learn from Jean Dale the great premium she consistently put on her love for people. He summoned her to her heavenly home on December 29, 2015 at the age of 95 and after 72½ years of marriage.

Grace and Jean Dale were very different. However, my mother and wife both influenced and blessed my life and did so in complementary ways. To my mother, I am indebted for a sense of the breadth of human life and divine thought and to Jean Dale for her love and sensitivity to people. They both loved and were committed deeply to Christ and the life to which He called them. They brought that love and commitment to my life as well. I deeply treasure and appreciate their love of Christ and their interconnected contributions to my life, to my family, and beyond.

# CONTENTS

# Foreword

*Your Gospel Is Too Small* could be an alternative title for this book. Many fascinating analyses await each reader, for it shows us that most people recognize only bits and pieces of the biblical accounts of the Good News. Dr. Jaggard encourages us to discern new ways of looking at the gospel through his emphasis upon two primary forms that, along with additional material, lead to a whole greater than its parts. Each form offers a distinct way of not only interpreting the gospel but also of personally claiming its truth.

Numerous questions are answered in the pages of Cedric's book. For example, are there biblical signposts for a broader view of the gospel than most Christians possess? In addition, what is the impact of knowing the plurality of New Testament descriptions of the gospel? How does such knowledge influence sin management? In what ways can we personally live out the distinctive forms of the Good News? Might clarifying it affect the church and help to bridge the destructive divisions in Christianity?

Written by one of the now rare survivors who personally studied under such notable theological giants as Karl Barth, Reinhold Niebuhr, and Paul Tillich, this account nevertheless is not by a disciple of any of them. Neither is it loaded with theological jargon. Using ordinary language that lay Christians can understand, it aims to bring formal theology closer into tune with its biblical foundations in a way that is accessible to a wide spectrum of readers.

Jaggard confirms the fact that good theology will not in itself make people become better Christians, but it can make them more effective agents for Christ. While he was seeking a deeper theological understanding of biblical truths about the gospel, he discovered that it is the foundation for a more mature Christian faith. As his view of the gospel broadened, it became a source of a deeper and richer faith, a more relational Christianity, and a more God-centered perspective than he had previously experienced.

One can read *Claiming a Larger Gospel* from many perspectives, including those of a social or behavioral scientist such as me. Doing so will help readers to discover how differing theological viewpoints influence important relationships and differences among people. The book's stimulation of a well-trained human imagination will also strengthen many interpretations of research findings and reveal numerous hypotheses to test in further scientific studies.

The gospel throws much light on people's understanding of themselves and their relationships with others. The triune nature of the "one God in three persons" (Father, Son, and Holy Spirit) is reflected in the analogous nature of human beings created in His image. Every person has a body, mind, and spirit or soul. Yet each is distinctly unique. Each has his or her way of being, believing, behaving, and belonging, which in turn are major categories of scientific investigation. All people base their lives on a usually unscripted set of assumptions and presuppositions that serve as their guide for living in the society and groups of which they are a part.

Recognition of the diverse forms of the gospel contributes to the awareness that there is a variety of approaches to spiritual growth. The gospel deepens faith, and it improves the ability to confront the devil's guises. It also helps us to cope with social conflicts and to adjust to transformations of society.

The stamp of theology is also prominent in society at large. In the early history of the United States of America, the biblical teaching that all people are sinners, even devout believers in Jesus Christ, was a major source of the now renowned separation of powers into the government's legislative, executive, and judicial branches. The spiritual importance of freedom of conscience played a role in the Constitution's freedom of religion and separation of church and state. Those in turn contributed significantly to the importation, invention, and adaptation of a variety of religions with their respective denominations, sects, and cults as well as to the emergence of countless pseudo-religious philosophies, self-improvement programs, healing cults, and "spiritual" guides. Fully understanding any of those movements and groups, as well as American society as a whole, is impossible without an appreciation of their theology-related philosophical foundations.

Theology is thus an important causal factor with significant interdisciplinary impacts relevant to all humanity and every person's life. The study of its pervasive presence and profound effects constitutes a huge domain of under-investigated topics in the social and behavioral sciences of religion. In contrast, ignoring its influence upon both the well-being and the problems of people and society leaves a huge gap, a void that contributes to behavioral and structural flaws of humanity instead of to constructive improvements.

Theology is no longer known as Queen of the Sciences, the collective label that then was applied to all of the ordered bodies of knowledge. However, it still is quietly interwoven into just about all human endeavors. One's view of God or belief in no god subtly influences every other area of life as part of one's worldview. Understanding the nuances among forms of the gospel often clarifies people's behavior. It helps explain and enriches many puzzling statements and theories of scientists, philosophers, other scholars, and ordinary people. Amorphous and formal theologies lie at the heart of daily life.

After six decades of teaching and research in the sociology of religion, I therefore have come to the conclusion that those that descriptively or analytically study humanity without paying at least some attention to theology are missing so much that they are derelict in their duties. Social scientists, philosophers, and other humanities scholars, as well as counselors and advisers, supervisors, and managers, who neglect the implicit and explicit contributions of theology to both the well-being and the troubles of people and society, are doing themselves and their followers a distinct disservice.

As clarified in this book, the gospel is the driving force behind Christianity. Offered to all humanity, it is the "Good News" about Jesus Christ. Details about that Good News can be viewed in diverse ways, few of which make it inconsequential. Cedric's careful study allows for a variety of interpretative models, each of which symbiotically coexists alongside the others, all mutually enriching each other.

*Claiming* contributes to an appreciation of the complications that arise from theological variations in the discovery and interpretations of biblical truths at the center of Christianity, the world religion with the most adherents. Many of the differences seem miniscule and inconsequential to outsiders, but even the minutiae

11

have contributed to endless study and ideological battles. Among the results are the emergence of competing sects and denominations with their diverse organizational adaptations, creeds, activities, and leadership styles. Theology is thus a major source of the rich mosaic of diverse religious subcultures in "the land of the free and the home of the brave."

Several years ago, Cedric was the principal founder of the Theological Confab, an informal discussion group that continues to meet monthly, sometimes with topics in this book as its focus of attention. Although he now is homebound because of physiological limitations, he continues to collaborate in its meetings via distance communication, usually adding perceptive comments to its conversations.

An additional perspective on this insightful analysis of interpretive types of the gospel comes from my role as a social gerontologist. On November 25, 2015, while still polishing the manuscript of this book, Cedric became a centenarian. Despite deterioration of his hearing and eyesight, his mind is clear, his memory is good, and his knowledge of the Bible is superb. He illustrates the fact that keeping one's mind actively engaged while aging helps immensely to delay or inhibit the mental deterioration that afflicts far too many senior adults after their seventieth or eightieth birthdays. He is an outstanding example of the elders taught by God from their youth who continue declaring his wondrous deeds and power, bearing fruit in old age (See Ps. 71:17–18, 92:12–15).

Reading this book reveals new forms and inspiring implications of the gospel. It helps us identify deceptive blind spots about who we really are, and it suggests a variety of possibilities for our own spiritual growth. Most of all, it enriches our appreciation of Jesus Christ, so it offers each of us much to gain and nothing to lose. Enjoy the book's intellectual and spiritual stimulation!

David O. Moberg, Ph.D.
Professor of Sociology Emeritus
Marquette University

# Preface

At a theological gathering I attended, someone asked the question: "What, in a word, is the gospel?" More than one participant responded, "Jesus died for our sins."

I believe the beloved people at that gathering would not deny the reality of Jesus' joyous resurrection, so their answers made me wonder: Should not any succinct statement of the gospel reflect the core meaning of the word "gospel", which is "good news"? Should not any summary of the gospel include both sides of teachings that the Apostle Paul identified as "of first importance"? Namely, "that Christ died for our sins in accordance with the scriptures, and that he was buried, and that he was raised on the third day in accordance with the scriptures" (1 Cor. 15:3–4 NRSV).

Centering either piety or theology too heavily on the cross alone can and has sometimes created an unfortunate misplacement of emphasis. The "good news" or "glad tidings" inherent in the definition and tone of the gospel can be obscured when people become preoccupied with the tragic nature of Jesus' death. Sadly, sometimes people do isolate Jesus' cross from his resurrection, and this can distort both their experience and sharing of the gospel message.

Happily, every serious Christian aspires to grow in faith, and this book speaks to that aspiration. I write this book in dialogue with other writers because, in recent years, several remarkable studies have focused on growth in faith. Significantly, what these studies have in common is that they center on practices in the Christian life—activities and exercises that we can refer to as "discipleship." As valuable as such explorations of practices are, they can underemphasize the value of comprehending the word "gospel" itself, along with the various forms in which the gospel can be expressed. Therefore, in this work, I seek to present a complementary emphasis on comprehension, by means of which we can love God with our minds in the context of our whole loves. See Jesus' summary of the law in Matthew 22:36–40.

With our goals of growth and comprehension in mind, we do well to survey some less than comprehensive versions of the gospel that may distort our own understanding and which we can grow beyond. Some people assume that the good news points to a one-time event in our lives. Although feeling deeply grateful, it lives on only in our memory. However, this one-sided emphasis based on a one-time event needs teachings that bring out the lifelong character of growth in Christ. Distorted versions of the gospel might include presentations promising worldly advantages that are self-serving rather than God-serving, testimonies emphasizing "how it happened to me" making one's own story normative for everyone, and "evangelistic" presentations seeking initial "religious" responses to the good news while ignoring how the gospel speaks to all spheres of life.

Without condemning those who hold to such incomplete versions of the gospel, we can seek to comprehend God's redemptive acts in ways that govern the fullness of worship and the wholeness of life. With respect to the fullness of worship, we can go beyond an initial "altar call", and we can encounter our Lord in worship that is both individual and corporate, including the Lord's Supper. With respect to the wholeness of life, we can serve our Lord not only in church on Sundays but in every activity and relationship in our everyday lives. As we claim this larger gospel, we will receive help from academic theologians, Christian apologists, philosophers, and all kinds of wise members in the body of Christ. In so doing, we will find the Scriptures offering us a larger and richer gospel in compelling ways.

Encouraging encounters of the gospel are also part of my story. I was humbled to find that those listening and responding in such helpful ways were not trained theologians or highly sophisticated scholars. They were deeply sincere in seeking to grow in faith and therefore wide open to looking at the Scriptures in a fresh way.

As I seek in this book to claim a larger gospel, I have these friends and acquaintances in mind. I will seek to write in a way that speaks to both lay Christians and theologians, and I will seek to equip both these groups to act as witnesses and even ambassadors to those who do not yet profess faith in Christ. Offering a larger gospel can make for growth in the body of Christ.

My story includes not only the personal conversations mentioned above but also ministry relationships that developed within my work as preacher and pastor in various settings. My ministry has included service to students, people with special needs, people in the military, and people living overseas. In carrying out work in such diverse settings, I found my own thinking stretched in a particular direction, namely, combining what we can call "the apostolic gospel" of Paul and other New Testament writers with what we can call "the kingdom gospel" proclaimed and embodied by Jesus himself.

As we will explore further in the body of the book, the apostolic gospel emphasizes the cross and resurrection of Christ, while the kingdom gospel emphasizes Jesus' ministry in Galilee, which includes works on Earth that relate to everything we do in this life. As I dealt with all kinds of people in all kinds of situations, I found myself led to ferret out Jesus' message in a way that speaks to the complex problems with which people live. I came to realize that many Christians have narrowed the apostolic gospel by centering only on the cross, while others have ignored the kingdom gospel by focusing only on the cross and resurrection. Such a shrinkage amounts to an injustice not only to the gospel itself but also to the people who hear it. We need Jesus' own proclamation of the good news to expand our life in Christ.

One illuminating example of expanding our life in Christ can be found in the work of the late philosopher-theologian Dallas Willard. This professor at the University of Southern California spoke to both the church and the world in books such as *The Divine Conspiracy* and *The Great Omission.*

In these and other works, Willard notes how people on both ends of the theological spectrum can reduce the gospel to what he calls versions of "sin management." By that term, he means, on the one hand, people focus almost exclusively on the forgiveness of individual sins that assures individuals they will go to heaven when they die. On the other hand, people can seek to manage sin by focusing only on fighting structural evils with no attention to transforming one's own character. On the basis of the Scriptures, Willard finds a way to preserve the truths of these two parties while also uniting and expanding on them. In this way, Willard makes an important contribution to how we offer the gospel to the world around us.    In my book I will carry out a similar mission.

By working in such a manner, I will also speak to those whose thinking has been filtered by the Fundamentalist–Modernist controversy that has consumed American religion for decades and continues to work powerfully under the surface of our differences today.  Fundamentalists tend to err in the direction of narrowing the apostolic gospel by concentrating exclusively on the forgiveness of individual sins. Modernists tend to err in the direction of narrowing the kingdom gospel by concentrating exclusively on structural evil.  Such partisan views weaken both biblical interpretation and other forms of scholarship, and they call us to open ourselves further to the breathing and blowing of the Holy Spirit.

## Note - Roman Catholic and Anglican Readers

In talking with Roman Catholic friends, I regularly find an understanding of the term "gospel" that differs from how Protestants use the word.  In the Roman Catholic Sunday Mass, there are assigned Bible readings in three categories: 1) Old Testament, 2) Acts or letters of the apostles and the rest of the New Testament, and 3) Gospel.  In that setting, "Gospel" is understood as referring to the four literary documents: Matthew,

Mark, Luke, and John.    That is not the way that Protestants use the term "gospel."    To express a similar thought, Protestants would always say "gospels" (plural).    Where Protestants commonly use the word "gospel", they refer to the gospel message that is scattered through the books of the New Testament. The term "gospel" as referring to a message rather than to literary documents is employed, for instance, by Paul at the opening of 1 Corinthians and in other passages. This difference is not a case of one tradition being right and the other wrong, but simply a difference of usage. This difference in usage may apply to Anglican readers as well. In this work, I will refer to the gospel as message with a lowercase "g" while referring to Gospel as document with an uppercase "G."

# PART 1
## Two Main Forms of the Gospel

## Chapter 1

## Introductory Directions and Definitions Regarding "Gospel"

"Long ago God spoke to our ancestors in many and various ways by the prophets, but in these last days he has spoken to us by a Son, whom he appointed heir of all things, through whom he also created the worlds. He is the reflection of God's glory and the exact imprint of God's very being, and he sustains all things by his powerful word. When he had made purification for sins, he sat down at the right hand of the Majesty on high, having become as much superior to angels as the name he has inherited is more excellent than theirs." (Hebrews 1:1–4 NRSV).

### Perplexities as Entryways

*Claiming a Larger Gospel* emerges from and adds to centuries of dialogue and debate regarding the essential teachings and events of the gospel. The book also reflects movements taking place around the world in our own time. In the paradoxical plan of God, it turns out that perplexities about the gospel can lead us into challenging studies that bear good fruit in our lives as Christians.

In terms of history, in the past two or three centuries, skepticism regarding the gospel has often come from people seeking to escape the confines of faith in order to engage in other issues. Thinkers in the tradition of Voltaire often felt that the eradication of altar and throne would lead to a more enlightened and humane society. Therefore, arguments about and against the gospel often took place among people seeking to escape religion and the church. My book will speak to such critiques indirectly because a true understanding of the gospel leads to enlightenment and liberation in which any honest seeker can share.

More recently, in the past hundred years or so, dialogue and debate have also taken place within and among the various traditions in the church. Although these conversations can take a scrappy and divisive tone, they can also bear good fruit. When carried out with an irenic spirit, ecumenical discussions can help us all avoid miscarriages of the gospel as we develop an open mind regarding its fullness. While serious debates remain necessary for the sake of truth, we can seek to always communicate in a constructive manner. I believe the gospel is so central to the life and growth of the body of Christ that all of us who confess Christ need to listen to the contributions of others. This is my hope for the millennium into which we have now entered.

As I offer my contribution to the dialogue, I join those who research and write in a spirit not of defensiveness but of creative self-criticism. In my search for a larger gospel, I have found help particularly with regard to Jesus' proclamation of the Kingdom of God. Writers who have widened my understanding of the gospel include Dallas Willard, whom I mentioned above, and also Richard Foster and Scot McKnight. Pastor-writers include Tim Keller, John Piper, and others whom I have encountered via the Internet. I have benefitted in particular from George Eldon Ladd's careful scholarly work regarding biblical concepts of the Kingdom, so I recommend both his scholarly work, *The Presence of the Future* (1974, a revised version of his book in 1964, *Jesus and the Kingdom: The Eschatology of Biblical Realism*), and his more popular title, *The Gospel of the Kingdom: Scriptural Studies.* Exploring these writers and related works can help us discover common biblical material and, therefore, live out Paul's teaching in Ephesians 4:3, in which he tells us to "make every effort to maintain the unity of the Spirit through the bond of peace."

In terms of geography, the post-World War II world opened a new era in global Christianity. Europe, which was at one time a leading fortress (for good and ill) on behalf of Christendom, saw a rapid and radical decline in church life. The church has not disappeared and the gospel continues to leaven European society, but that continent stands in need of deep spiritual reinvigoration. With important adaptations, the same observation applies to North America. Canada has followed the European pattern fairly closely. The United States has had much surface Christianity, but a lack of roots has led to withering. Mexico also would benefit from Christian renewal, in settings both Roman Catholic and Protestant.

At the same time, the gospel has taken on new life in nations such as China and Iran and in various nations that we once called the Third World. Africa and Asia were once targets for Christian outreach, and they have now become sources of Christian missionaries. Turmoil in the Near East prompts us to engage in both historical studies and responsible use of contemporary means of communication. So in order to heed the call of the gospel to our time and place, I will begin with a study of the word "gospel" itself. In this way, I will engage in what people call "biblical" (as distinguished from "systematic") theology.

## Meaning and Usage of "Gospel" and "Good News" (The Meaning of the Word "Gospel")

Gerhard Kittel's highly regarded *Theological Dictionary of the New Testament* provides, in English translation, a distinctly helpful analysis of the term *euaggelion,* the Greek word translated "gospel" or "the good news." I include selective comments, here and elsewhere, that I have found pertinent and helpful. This word study helps us understand Jesus, who is not only one who proclaims the gospel message but actually is himself the good news from God.

In the New Testament, the first three Gospels—Matthew, Mark, and Luke—are often referred to as "the Synoptic Gospels." The word "synoptic" connotes looking together at one person or event, which the first three Gospels often do. Scholars generally view Mark as the first Gospel to appear in written form. Matthew and Luke each relied on Mark, along with other sources, and these three Gospels have much overlap in content. The fourth Gospel, John, offers a perspective on Jesus so different that people often refer to John as "the maverick Gospel." In this section, we will focus on the Synoptic Gospels.

The first half of all three Synoptic Gospels reaches a climax in Peter's confession at Caesarea Philippi. In response to Jesus' question, "Who do people say that the Son of Man is"? Simon Peter responds, "You are the Messiah (or "the Christ" (KJV); "Messiah" is the Hebrew word for "Anointed", while "Christ" is the Greek word), the Son of the Living God." (Matthew 16:13, Matt. 16:16; cf. Mark 8:29 and Luke 9:20). In common practice, the English translation for the Greek *euaggelion* can be either "gospel" or "good news", words that can be used interchangeably. I see the *euaggelion* as referring to the anticipated Anointed One, the Messiah King prophesied in the Old Testament. Jesus was still largely unidentified, and had a secret identity until He entered the lives of the Jewish people in Galilee. In unexpected yet fulfilling ways, Jesus reveals a long-awaited promise of a much anticipated Messiah King. Any presentation of the gospel message that reflects the New Testament Gospels will have Jesus the Messiah at its center. Without Jesus at its center, the word "gospel" loses its biblical meaning and the good news God has for the human family.

**New Testament Usage of the Term "Good News"**

Although the word "gospel" has come, rightly, to refer to Jesus and his message, it is important to note that in the days of Jesus' earthly ministry, the term had a variety of meanings. For example, as Jesus preached, taught, and healed throughout Galilee and Judea, the overall political control of that region was under the rule of the Roman Empire, which stretched over much of the known world during that time. The land that was also called "Israel" was geographically divided into two different parts: Judea, with the capital city of Jerusalem, which enjoyed a certain amount of independent control, especially over the religious life of Jews along with their everyday practices, and Galilee, a province farther north where Jesus did most of his public ministry. In between Judea and Galilee lay Samaria, which had had complicated relations with Judea over a period of centuries and, in the days of Jesus, was radically estranged from both Judea and Galilee. Going from Galilee to Judea was not a generally pleasant experience for the Jewish people, but Samaria could hardly be avoided if traveling by land when going from one to the other. And because all faithful Jews were encouraged to be present at the annual Passover feast held in Jerusalem, along with other feasts, the dangerous journey had to take place on a regular basis. (For an example in Jesus' ministry, see Luke 9:51–55). References, particularly in the Gospel of John, to Jesus' visits to the festivals largely are responsible for many Bible scholars' estimates of the three and a half years of Jesus' public ministry as a whole.

Important for this study is that for many Christians, their understanding of the gospel message is typically based only on what came to be called the Apostolic Gospel, meaning sometimes the cross and resurrection

27

of Jesus, but even more often just the cross alone.   On the other hand, the term "gospel" appears prominently in the description of Jesus' activity in most of that time period in Galilee, where frequent references to the good news clearly appear in a very different form.   It is not immediately clear how these two forms may affect each other in how we present the gospel today, which is a major reason I have written this book.   I would like to explore with the readers the Scripture passages that suggest we have been overlooking sections of the Scriptures that could enable Christians to find, and share with others, a larger and more comprehensive description of our Lord and the good news he both preaches and incarnates.

Such a renewed study of biblical passages speaks to many contemporary issues that can hinder the church in North America.   In the United States especially, life in the church has been fraught with controversy, even schisms within denominations, with seemingly ineffective efforts to recover the lost unity of the church.       Efforts to bring forward more irenic approaches have often been quickly dismissed as "selling out to the opposite side."   In response to this sadly polemical setting Dallas Willard and others have deplored the consequent discouragement of "give-and-take scholarship", which could open doors to reconciliation and unity.   Willard and several others with similar perspectives have raised hope for unity by posing questions about the Christian life of discipleship. By focusing on discipleship as opposed to speculative arguments, students of the gospel can bring new life not only to new believers but also to lifelong Christians. Many of these ecumenical writers have made worthwhile insights that we cannot afford to overlook. Nevertheless, other truths remain to be explored. One particular problem to date has been the difficulty of meshing the Apostolic Gospel (as summarized by Paul in 1 Corinthians 15:1–11) with the good news of the Kingdom of God (as proclaimed by Jesus in the portraits found in the Synoptic Gospels). Therefore, in this book, we will both explore these two forms of the gospel and also take steps to unite them into a whole that is greater than its parts.

For the gospel to be complete, should we not explore the wide array of biblical passages that express the good news? In the chapters that follow, we will explore the wealth of gospel terminology and expressions, and we will bring our conclusions together to deepen our understanding of the good news of Jesus the Messiah.

## Overt and Latent Gospel: A Theme That Emerges

One major theme in this book merits mention now because it is central to the book's goal of helping us claim a larger gospel. Briefly stated, the theme goes as follows: To arrive at a scriptural picture of the gospel, we need to consider two types of material. *Overt gospel* is that which is openly called "gospel" and for the most part is not difficult to identify; *latent gospel* is physically located apart from other references to gospel material yet can be significant for our understanding of the good news. Marks of the latent gospel can be more difficult to ferret out, but I will draw some of them to your attention and alert you to look for them throughout the Scriptures. In this way, we can find patterns either similar or complementary to the more numerous examples of the overt gospel. Taken together, the overt and latent expressions of the gospel amount to a whole greater than its parts.

# Chapter 2

# The Apostolic (Pauline) Proclamation

"Now I would remind you, brothers and sisters, of the good news that I proclaimed to you, which you in turn received, in which also you stand, through which also you are being saved, if you hold firmly to the message that I proclaimed to you—unless you have come to believe in vain. For I handed on to you as of first importance what I in turn had received: that Christ died for our sins in accordance with the scriptures, and that he was buried, and that he was raised on the third day in accordance with the scriptures." (1 Corinthians 15:1–4 NRSV).

**Introduction and Overview**

As mentioned above, one way to analyze New Testament testimonies regarding Christ is to recognize two major presentations of the gospel: first, the preaching of Jesus himself and second, the proclamation of the Apostle Paul.

Chronologically and theologically, it might seem fitting to begin our study by beginning with Jesus and his proclamation of the Kingdom of God. Jesus died and rose before Paul began his apostolic ministry, and Jesus is the gospel, while Paul is merely a servant (or even a "slave") of our Lord. In fact, the Apostle Paul himself testifies that when he arrived at Corinth to preach the gospel, he "decided to know nothing among you except Jesus Christ, and him crucified."  (1 Corinthians 2:2). Later in his Corinthian correspondence, Paul wrote, "We do not proclaim ourselves; we proclaim Jesus Christ as Lord and ourselves as your slaves for Jesus' sake." (2 Corinthians 4:5 NRSV).  So why should we begin with Paul's apostolic proclamation of the gospel rather than with Jesus himself?

For one thing, even though Jesus' earthly ministry preceded Paul's chronologically, Paul's epistles were written to the churches before the written Gospels were composed.  So in the realm of the written word, the Apostle Paul precedes the evangelists Matthew, Mark, Luke, and John.  In addition to that chronological note, we can also observe that when people summarize the gospel, they often—whether knowingly or not—follow a Pauline pattern.  As mentioned above, many Christians summarize the gospel by saying, "Jesus died for our sins."  In that summary, they could appeal to Paul's example in 1 Corinthians 2:2.  So in this book, we will begin where people are by beginning with Paul, and we will lead people via Paul to a larger understanding of the Lord.

Many scholars recognize Paul's epistle to the Romans as his fullest expression of the gospel, and some Christians would point to Romans Chapter 3 as providing a succinct statement of the gospel. As Paul seeks to unite Jews and Gentiles into one new humanity in Christ, he writes, "For there is no distinction, since all have sinned and fall short of the glory of God; they are now justified by his grace as a gift, through the redemption that is in Christ Jesus." (Romans 3:22–24 NRSV). Others could make the case for Romans 1:16 as a summary of the gospel since it uses the word "gospel" and presents the good news as "the power of God for the salvation of everyone who has faith, to the Jew first and also to the Greek." In my own view, the first eight chapters of Romans as a whole express central truths of the gospel, especially in terms of revealing the universality of sin, which the gospel must address in order to bring salvation. However, as rich as the material of Romans is, I propose Paul's central summary of the gospel comes in 1 Corinthians 15:1–4, which reads as follows:

> "Now I would remind you, brothers and sisters, of the good news that I proclaimed to you, which you in turn received, in which also you stand, through which also you are being saved, if you hold firmly to the message that I proclaimed to you—unless you have come to believe in vain. For I handed on to you as of first importance what I in turn had received: that Christ died for our sins in accordance with the

scriptures, and that he was buried, and that he was raised on the third day in accordance with the scriptures." (1 Corinthians 15:1–4 NRSV)

This passage contains much that is central to the gospel. For one thing, it includes the term "euaggelion", or "gospel." In addition, it refers to salvation and to Jesus Christ. Importantly, it refers not only to Christ dying for our sins but it also gives equal emphasis to Christ rising on the third day. And finally, Paul refers to these teachings as "of first importance." When he writes that he "handed on" what he "received", he further indicates that this was the gospel the other apostles preached since the day of Pentecost, when Peter preached that God's people had crucified God's Son and yet "God raised him up" (Acts 2:24). By packing all that central material into four brief verses, Paul offers us an excellent summary of the gospel. This passage, along with other passages in Paul's epistles, offers us material seeking church unity rather than disunity, and it gives a biblical basis for a gospel that is rich and compelling.

### Excursus: Paul—Theologian or Apostle?

As we turn to the Apostle Paul to understand the gospel, it is worth noting that scholars have sometimes debated whether Paul qualifies as a genuine theologian or not. Those with reservations about him as a theologian can refer to a seemingly unfinished gospel summary in 1 Corinthians 15, which breaks off from its succinct list of gospel components and devotes the long remainder of the chapter in our Bibles to a powerful treatment of just one of the components, namely, the resurrection. It is not an exaggeration to say that this chapter is the single most significant listing of the resurrection appearances that we have in Scriptures. Further, it adds much to our understanding of the resurrection by bringing out the implications both in relation to Jesus' work and to our lives. Also, the preceding verses of the chapter constitute the fullest statement of any form of overt gospel, although Paul does require the reader to go to his more worshipful gospel summary in Romans 1:1–8, in which he brings out the ongoing application and expansion of the gospel through the work of the Holy Spirit (who is not mentioned in the gospel summary at the opening of 1 Corinthians 15).

In order to receive Paul's message, we can observe that after his life-changing conversion on the road to Damascus, he did not at once plunge into an evangelistic mission of church planting and writing, although he did some earlier preaching. A period of unknown duration, both as to parts and to the whole, likely served for his own discipleship and preparation for the apostolic ministry to which God had called him (Romans 1:1)— part of the time in Arabia and three years in Damascus itself. (For Paul's own biographical narrative regarding this time, see Galatians 1:11–24). At the end of that reflective time, Paul returned to Jerusalem, and during a time of intense prayer, he was given a warning from Jesus regarding limiting his time in Jerusalem (See Acts 22:17–21). In 1 Corinthians 9, Paul describes the responsibilities, the sacrifices, and sometimes the rewards of his apostolic vocation.

Interestingly, the editors of both the NRSV and the NIV do not include the word "gospel" in the titles they assign to 1 Corinthians 15. Even though the more comprehensive term "gospel" is prominent in the chapter, the editors of both give us a title around just one part of the gospel. In titling the chapter, they had to choose between two features, each of immense importance: the overt gospel as a whole and the nature of the Resurrection, a critical component of the gospel (which has been frequently viewed as secondary and only auxiliary to the Cross). Rather than making some reference to the gospel as a whole, the editors of both translations title the chapter "The Resurrection of Christ." In this way, they fail to reflect the fullness of Paul's message.

Many of Christ's post-resurrection appearances are mentioned in Scripture only in 1 Corinthians 15. In that chapter, Paul distinguishes between what he calls the natural or physical human body prior to Jesus' resurrection and what he calls the spiritual body, which we will receive as participants in God's resurrection harvest. When Jesus rose, he appeared as a "first fruits" (1 Corinthians 15:20) to many of his followers individually, in small groups, and once to over five hundred people. The harvest metaphor in the chapter, which proclaims that "Christ has been raised from the dead, the first fruits of those who have died", gives us a way to visualize the promise of what will one day take place in the lives of all believers. By speaking in such a way, we can agree with John Stott that whether we view Paul as a theologian or not, we can certainly see him as a visionary Christian thinker, who opens minds to the call of theology as either an academic discipline or as a way to pray and act in thoughtful ways.

We can note further that the role of theologian is not a biblical concept, but has developed over the years as Christians have endeavored to express their faith in harmony with the Scriptures as a whole. Therefore, it is not surprising that while Paul does not refer to himself as a theologian, he is in no way hesitant to call himself an apostle. His most fulsome treatise on the good news, the first eight chapters of Romans, begins with these words: "Paul, a servant of Jesus Christ, called to be an apostle, *set apart for the gospel of God*" (Romans 1:1 NRSV; italics are my own). His contribution as an apostle, expressly as an apostle of the gospel, is far more important than his sometimes ad hoc arrangements of theological material, as some theologians of today might view it. Moreover, Paul, in his letters and in his work as a whole, is seldom very far from the gospel as a whole. For example, he clearly expresses his desire (to the Ephesian elders) to declare the whole "counsel of God" (Act 20:27 KJV), which must include the fullness of good news—not the cross alone, not the resurrection alone, but the entire saving act of God, with all that led up to and follows it.

Related to these observations is the further truth that when Paul's epistles deal with the Christian life introduced by the gospel rather than the gospel message itself, the Apostle's tone is much like Jesus' holistic call for gospel acceptance—especially as reported by John. In his dialogue with Nicodemus, Jesus states "that whoever believes in him may have eternal life." (John 3:15 NRSV). Paul echoes his Lord when, speaking to a jailer in Philippi, he says in the imperative voice, "Believe on the Lord Jesus, and you will be saved." That brief statement of the gospel led to a whole new way of life for the jailer and his household. (See Acts 16:25-40).

We cannot very well fault Paul for his not being what we would think of as a fully consistent theologian in an academic sense. Like other intellectual and academic disciplines, theology developed and refined over time. We can think, for example, of how the ancient Greek historian Herodotus would not qualify as a historian in today's strict academic sense. Thucydides built on the work of Herodotus, coming closer to modern standards, but even in his case, the discipline has developed. Since theology as the highly refined discipline we know today was not in existence, we may, with some restrictions, speak of the theology of the Old Testament, of the New Testament, or of applying the discipline we know of as theology to such themes. In doing so, we may better grasp the context and the force of such passages. With Paul's historical context in mind, let's explore his visionary message further.

## Reconciliation

In regard to Paul's proclamation in 1 Corinthians 15:1–4, we can speak of an "overt" presentation of the gospel. (See the section in chapter one regarding overt and latent expressions of the gospel). To use the term "overt" here is to say that we can see Paul using the word "gospel" as he proclaims the gospel message. In addition to such overt presentations of the gospel, Paul—along with other New Testament writers—also offers what we can call not a "covert" presentation, but rather a "latent" presentation in the sense that some of his material sleeps, so to speak, in people's minds because they give it insufficient attention until they wake up to the fullness and implications of the gospel message.

When we turn to "latent" presentations of the gospel, we find that gospel at work not only when we see the actual word "gospel" but also when the gospel works like a seed growing secretly. In other words, like his Lord Jesus, Paul can proclaim a message that sprouts and grows even when, like the farmer in Jesus' parable, "he does not know how." (Mark 4:27 NRSV). Two major examples of this latent yet fruit-bearing presentation of the gospel come to mind, which we can place under the rubrics "reconciliation" and "transformation." We will deal first with reconciliation and then devote a brief section to transformation.

With respect to Paul and reconciliation, we can begin with the biblical book that many scholars view as Paul's first written epistle, namely, his letter to the Galatians. Galatians may seem an unlikely place to begin to explore reconciliation since Paul begins the letter with a fierce denunciation of rival teachers who are seeking to lead the Galatians toward a different gospel. According to Paul, there is no other gospel, and therefore, he writes, "As we have said before, so now I repeat, if anyone proclaims to you a gospel contrary to what you received, let that one be accursed!" (Galatians 1:9 NRSV).

But the truth behind Paul's ferocious defense of the gospel is that he opposes any addition to the reality of Christ alone as the Savior we need and who brings us reconciliation with God.    For Paul, to make even God's law as revealed to Moses a necessary addition for salvation in Christ is to deny the grace and truth of Christ.    Therefore, in a self-revealing testimony to Christ as Savior, Paul writes, "And the life I now live in the flesh I live by faith in the Son of God, who loved me and gave himself for me.    I do not nullify the grace of God, for if justification comes through the law, then Christ died for nothing."   (Galatians 2:20–21 NRSV).

Having expressed his own feelings of devotion, gratitude, and even awe in relation to Christ, Paul goes on to indicate his passionate and painful love for his fellow believers in Galatia.  As he calls the Galatians back to the true gospel and the only Savior, Paul states, "My little children, for whom I am again in the pain of childbirth until Christ is formed in you, I wish I were present with you now and could change my tone, for I am perplexed about you."    (Galatians 4:19–20 NRSV). With that statement and throughout Galatians, Paul reveals his desire for reconciliation with God to translate into reconciliation among humans.

The further truth is this:  for the sake of Christ and his reconciliation, Paul is prepared not only to endure pain but even to die.  (See Philippians 1:12–26). For the Apostle, Christ is worthy of any sacrifice since he is the hinge on which history turns in God's plan to form one new humanity.    Speaking in relation to his fellow

Jews, Paul writes, "But when the fullness of time had come, God sent his Son, born of a woman, born under the law, so that we might receive adoption as children. And because you are children, God has sent the Spirit of his Son into our hearts, crying, 'Abba! Father!' So you are no longer a slave but a child, and if a child then also an heir, through God." (Galatians 4:4–7 NRSV). And part of the inheritance from God is reconciliation with people from every background.

Having described Christ as bringing adoption and freedom to Jews, Paul also proclaims Gentiles as sharing in the inheritance and the salvation that God promises. For Paul, the inclusion of Gentiles (non-Jews from every nation) in the family of faith goes all the way back to promises God made to Abraham. In Galatians 3, Paul refers to promises God makes in Genesis 12, Genesis 18, and Genesis 22. He writes, "And the scripture, foreseeing that God would justify the Gentiles by faith, declared the gospel beforehand to Abraham saying, 'All the Gentiles shall be blessed in you'. For this reason, those who believe are blessed with Abraham who believed." (Galatians 3:8–9 NRSV).

Implied in Paul's overt use of the word "gospel" in Galatians is a latent expression of the gospel in terms of reconciliation. For Paul, the gospel takes true expression only when Jews and Gentiles sit at one table, communing with the Christ who reconciled them both to

God. (See Galatians 2:11–21). The same God who had temporarily separated his chosen Jewish people from every nation (Galatians 3:19–29) now unites Jews and Gentiles as one people—one people who receive life from the Holy Spirit of Christ and who now, together, walk by the Spirit. (Galatians 5:25). Jewish and Gentile believers, like all believers in Christ, can practice reconciliation toward one another because "neither circumcision nor uncircumcision is anything; but a new creation is everything"! (Galatians 6:15 NRSV). In this new creation, we can all live out the joy of reconciliation, which is a major, although latent, expression of the gospel.

Having implied reconciliation in his epistle to the Galatians, Paul expresses the theme more explicitly in his epistles to the Romans and the Ephesians. In a truly dramatic statement in Romans 5, Paul reveals the love of God in Christ leading to reconciliation. The Apostle states,

> "For while we were still weak, at the right time Christ died for the ungodly. Indeed, rarely will anyone die for a righteous person—though perhaps for a good person someone might actually dare to die. But God proves his love for us in that while we still were sinners Christ died for us. Much more surely

then, now that we have been justified by his blood, will we be saved through him from the wrath of God. For if while we were enemies, we were *reconciled* to God through the death of his Son, much more surely, having been reconciled, will we be saved by his life. But more than that, we even boast in God through our Lord Jesus Christ, through whom we have now received *reconciliation.*" (Romans 5:6–11 NRSV, italics added).

In his epistle to the Ephesians, Paul shows that the saving grace of God in Christ leads to a peace between Jews and Gentiles, which turns out to be paradigmatic for bonds of peace we can form among all groups. According to the gospel, different races, ethnicities, classes, genders, and political groups can keep their identities while also becoming one in Christ. According to Paul, such an astonishing unity sends a message of reconciliation to the entire cosmos. The reader can find an eloquent expression of this gospel claim in Ephesians 2–3, where the grace of Christ leads to the breaking down of walls of hostility. And when formerly alienated members of different groups gather together for worship, it helps everyone (including spiritual powers!) to see the embodiment of gospel reconciliation. Paul states that in Christ, God formed the church "to make everyone see what is the plan of the mystery hidden for ages in God who created all things; so that through the church the wisdom of God in its rich variety might now be made known to the rulers and authorities in the heavenly places." (Ephesians 3:9–10 NRSV). What good news to remember the next time we attend worship!

On the basis of the few passages explored above, we are certainly beginning to claim Paul's gospel message in a larger way since we are seeing how it implies reconciliation. A similar truth applies as we move now to transformation.

## Transformation and Responsibility

When it comes to the latent gospel implication of transformation, we find Paul's central passage in Romans 12. Having proclaimed the gospel profoundly in Romans 1–8, and having agonized over his fellow Jews while concluding with a doxology in Romans 9–11, Paul now turns to how we can live out the gospel in everything we do, whether we refer explicitly to the word "gospel" or not. Paul writes, "I appeal to you therefore, brothers and sisters, by the mercies of God, to present your bodies as a living sacrifice, holy and acceptable to God, which is your spiritual worship. Do not be conformed to this world, *but be transformed* by the renewing of your minds, so that you may discern what is the will of God — what is good and acceptable and perfect." (Romans 12:1–2 NRSV, italics added).

For Paul, the good news of Christ and the reconciliation we receive in Christ can and must transform us into people like Jesus Christ. Although Paul does not use the word "transformed" earlier in Romans, he does teach transformation—the perfection of our characters into Christ-likeness—in earlier passages, such as Romans 5 and Romans 8. In Romans 5, Paul teaches that we can glorify and enjoy God even when we suffer because God can use our suffering as a means of transformation. Paul writes that "suffering produces endurance, and endurance produces character, and character produces hope, and hope does not disappoint us, because God's love has been poured into our hearts through the Holy Spirit that has been given to us." (Romans 5:3–5 NRSV).

In Romans 8, Paul uses different terminology to make a related point regarding transformation into Christ-likeness. Here he writes, "For those whom [God] foreknew he also predestined to be *conformed to the image of his Son*, in order that he might be the firstborn within a large family. And those whom he predestined he also called; and those whom he called he also justified; and those whom he justified he also glorified." (Romans 8:29–30 NRSV, italics added). So if we want to find other passages in the apostolic message of Paul regarding transformation, we do well to keep our eyes open to a variety of terms, including "holiness" or, to call on a traditional theological term, "sanctification." Once we wake up to the variety of terms, we can find the theme of transformation in a passage such as Colossians where Paul writes, "And you who were once estranged and hostile in mind, doing evil deeds, he has now reconciled in his fleshly body through death, so as to present you holy and blameless and irreproachable before him—provided that you continue securely established and steadfast in the faith." (Colossians 1:21–23 NRSV).

We do well to attend to the Colossians 1 passage because it brings out the human role and responsibility in the latent gospel implication of transformation. As God transforms us—or, to use yet another related term—as God delivers us from an old life alien to God into a new life reconciled to God, our Lord calls us to such vital practices as discipleship, obedience, service, love, and praise. The transformation we experience in relation to the gospel does not occur only in our initial reception of the good news. In fact, it is not even fully completed in this present life. As we yearn for and receive a personal relationship with God the Father and our Lord Jesus Christ through the moving of the Holy Spirit, we receive not only such comforting experiences such as blessings and assurance; we receive also a transformation that sanctifies our entire selves and everything we do. And as we experience this rich transformation by means of the whole gospel for our whole lives in the whole world, we wind up joining Paul in the doxology that leads him to his transformation teachings in Romans 12. With the Apostle, we express our response to the gospel by singing, "O the depth of the riches and wisdom and knowledge of God!" (Romans 11:33 NRSV).

As we give attention to how transformation includes our human responsibility in the drama of salvation, we want to do two things at the same time: We want to maintain a theocentric gospel and theology, while also recognizing human dignity and responsibility. As God lavishes grace on us, God does not treat us as blocks of wood or machines. Instead, God liberates us to become fully and freely human in relation to Christ. Here are some thoughts and questions that occur to me and that I pass on to you as we ponder how salvation, reconciliation, transformation, and the fullness of the gospel is both God-centered and human-centered at the same time.

One thought that arises as we ponder the gospel has to do with living in our often sad and complicated world. Living as we do amidst profound needs that make up our human predicament, we treasure – understandably and rightly – the personal blessings and assurances that God provides for us as an outcome of the gospel in our lives. We find security from our fears in the assurances of life eternal with God. In the promises of God, many of them likely metaphorically expressed, we look forward to the ending of sorrow; to new bodies on the day of Resurrection for all believers; to living in a New Jerusalem; and to much more—more than we can even imagine. (See Ephesians 3:20-21). Such outcomes of the gospel, however variously understood, may be characterized as subjective in nature, and are part of the hope that frequently carries Christians through many of the difficulties we face in the present life.

Personal blessings have to do with not only our welfare but also a large range of spiritual blessings that we may personally begin to realize. How do we look at life, our world, our love life and friends, at the body of the Christian church? We think also of the beautiful catalogue of Christian experiences that Paul recites in a passage "the fruit of the Spirit is love, joy, peace, patience, kindness, generosity, faithfulness, gentleness, and self-control." (Galatians 5:22–23 NRSV). Such blessings can begin to enter the Christian's present life. Or there may be future personal spiritual blessings, such as, "Now I know only in part; then I will know fully, even as I have been fully known." (1 Corinthians 13:12 NRSV).

Another set of thoughts and questions that arise have to do with a deeply personal question: Can I be sure? What can we say and experience in regard to Christian certainty? Do we know or can we know that we belong to God through Christ? Some believe that it is presumptuous to make such an affirmation, but Paul surely spoke with certainty when he wrote, "I am not ashamed, for I know the one in whom I have put my trust, and I am sure that he is able to guard until that day what I have entrusted to him." (2 Timothy 1:12 NRSV). Paul further explains how such true certainty (as opposed to carnal presumption) comes about. He writes, "The Spirit Himself testifies with our spirit that we are children of God." (Romans 8:16 YLT).

It is a meeting of two spirits—Christ's Spirit and ours—that brings about this biblical assurance. However, while we may have every confidence in the human commitment of others, we must be very sure not to infringe upon the judgment of God and make ourselves the judge of others in any ultimate sense. We should share the gospel boldly as ambassadors for Christ, but we should allow the assurance of salvation for the recipient to be divinely generated rather than as a result of our words of certainty for him or her.

A striking example comes to my own recollection. Upon his election to church office, a long-time Christian believer received the assurance of his faith. In order to better handle his forthcoming responsibilities, among several preparatory steps, he took a course in public speaking. To the surprise of many, his effectiveness as a church leader was much enhanced by this unpredicted but God-ordained activity.

Still, such blessings and assurances constitute only a secondary part of the outcome of our salvation. The primary part lies in our relationship with God, the one to whom we belong. It is that relationship that exalts him and helps us understand who we are.

We must keep in mind that the central focus of the good news is first and foremost about what God has done and what he has promised he will do. Without the redemptive acts of God in Christ, there would be no gospel. In a relationship that clearly is centered in God, both the personal blessings and the defining of our salvation, in terms of to whom we belong, are real. But the latter definition must be given clear priority. The gospel is God-centered.

Among contemporary theologians, John Piper and others have stressed the great importance of a theocentric proclamation of the gospel. To this end, we cannot afford to miss the strong emphasis in the heart of the gospel (as a whole) on the action of God. In a sovereign and saving way, God responds to the most far-reaching of our human needs: the redemptive acts of God through his Son and the striking changes he effects in the divine–human relationship.    It is these divine actions that make our human responses possible.

To offer another passage that reflects this truth, we can look at 1 Corinthians 6:19–20, where Paul declares, "Or do you not know…that you are not your own?  For you were bought with a price."    In an effective way, isn't Paul stating here the very nature of our salvation? It was incorporated in one of the historic explanations of the Cross, known as the ransom theory.  This is rightly understood not as a ransom paid to Satan but as a necessity within the nature of God and his own veracity regarding the deadly nature of sin if forgiveness and justification are to be freely offered for humankind. Thus, in the supreme sense, our salvation rests in the one to whom we belong, and the one whose persons we are.    By his mighty acts of redemption, God's claim upon us is complete.    Recall the chorus from an old hymn:

> O victory in Jesus, My Savior, forever.
> He sought me and bought me
> with His redeeming blood.
> He loved me ere I knew Him,
> And all my love is due Him.
> He plunged me to victory
> beneath the cleansing flood.

It is at this point that a crucial call is made upon our faith. To whom, really, do I belong? Many see three options here: belonging to Christ, belonging to the evil one, or belonging to oneself. A moment of reflection on the Genesis story of the temptation of Adam and Eve: The temptation that Adam and Eve faced was cleverly disguised by the serpent as though it had nothing to do with the serpent himself but was between Adam, Eve and God. We may imagine that we can confront God neutrally when, actually, we are submitting to the deceptive allurements of the evil one. Our salvation is found in the one to whom we belong. The alternative to belonging to God is belonging to Satan. The deepest meaning of our salvation, above all personal blessings, is in our *relationship* with God. How does God become our salvation, and how do we come to belong to him? It is by at least one of his redemptive actions and by our response of faith, which itself is a gift from God. (Ephesians 2:8).

Are there three options of who will be lord and master of our lives—God, Satan, or ourselves? It is from this autonomy that so many of us have found it difficult to free ourselves. We want to be our own person, but the gospel summons us to be God's person (again, 1 Corinthians 6:19–20). The choice, however, is between two options, God and Satan. For it is the very voice of the evil one that disguises a call that comes from him as though it were a third or neutral option—a prime example of the way in which the evil one deviously works his way into our lives whenever he can.

The critical issue we have to decide is between God and the evil one's mastery of our lives. The pivotal nature of the 1 Corinthians 6:19–20 passage provides what is for many a crucial turning point in relation to Christ and the gospel. In the allegiance we choose for our lives, we have a choice between God and Satan. If we posit a third choice, namely allegiance to self, as though it were neutral to the other two, we fall into the very deception to which Adam and Eve succumbed. Thus, can there be any response to God's redemptive work or to the gospel, which is actually neutral? We are lured by a choice, which is satanically dominated, and thereby act as though we are God—in many ways, the prime sin of humankind. Satan utterly misleads with his denial of the consequences of disobeying God: "You will not die." (Genesis 3:4 NRSV). We will return to Genesis and the human predicament in a later chapter. For now, we want to simply note the theocentric character of the gospel in a way that does not erase human dignity and responsibility.

One outcome of our salvation embraces personal blessings and assurances (for now and eternity) that God cares for and always will care for those who belong to him: eternal life with him, a place prepared for us in the Father's house, the banishment of sorrow and tears, and numerous other assurances. Many find especially helpful the open-ended promises God brings, finding confidence and comfort in such expressions as the memorable ascription of praise (Ephesians 3:20 NIV)— "Now to him who is able to do immeasurably more than all we ask or imagine...to him be glory in the church and in Christ Jesus"—and in the promise of 1 Corinthians 2:9: "What no eye has seen, nor ear heard, nor the human heart conceived what God has prepared for those who love him." Is it not better to rest on such open-ended assurances rather than to expend energy debating on whether to expect that the streets of the new Jerusalem will be literally or figuratively of gold and the gates literally or figuratively of pearl?

It is on the basis of the primacy of God and his work as we find it in Scripture as a whole—in bringing about reconciliation and by his several acts of redemption through which he "bought" us, in transformation of our lives, and in our personal union with Christ—that God is primary, and we should always remember he is primary. The Bible is a book about God, the revelation about himself and his purposes for creation. It opens with "In the beginning God...." This center of gravity is one of the most important unifying factors, with Scripture revelation recounting his mighty acts of redemption through Christ. Paul expresses the implication of God-centeredness eloquently at the end of Romans 8, when he rhetorically shakes his fist at the powers of evil and asserts, "For I am convinced that neither death, nor life, nor angels, nor principalities, nor things present, nor things to come, nor powers, nor height, nor depth, nor anything else in all creation, will be able to separate us from the love of God in Christ Jesus our Lord." (Romans 8:38–39 NRSV).

On the basis of the character of the Bible as a whole, we are forced to give prime consideration to what God has done and to the passages that declare that centrality. The Bible closes with words about God's reigning forever and ever. It teaches that we were made by him, were made for his glory, and are to glorify him in all that we do. This primary relationship consequently finds ultimate expression in the believer's life with this encouragement: "So, whether you eat or drink, or whatever you do, do everything for the glory of God." (1 Corinthians 10:31 NRSV). Thus, even our personal blessings and assurances related to our human responsibility ultimately redound to the glory of God.

**Eschatology—In Part**

Before we conclude our brief overview of the apostolic gospel in both its overt and latent forms as we encounter them in the epistles of Paul, we do well to note a few passages having to do with eschatology, or "the last things." As Paul himself states, "If for this life only we have hoped in Christ, we are of all people most to be pitied." (1 Corinthians 15:19 NRSV). For Paul and other believers suffering persecution, this observation shines brightly against a dark background, and even for those of us enjoying much good in this life, the hope of a world better than we can imagine remains central to the gospel. (See Ephesians 3:20–21). So we can conclude our brief overview of Paul's message with a brief exploration of its ultimate hope.

In one of his letters to the Corinthians, the Apostle states, "See, now is the acceptable time; see, now is the day of salvation!" (2 Corinthians 6:2 NRSV). When Paul emphasizes the present experience of salvation, reconciliation, transformation, and other expressions of the gospel, he practices what theologians call "realized eschatology." Realized eschatology means God's gifts of eternal life and new creation have broken into our lives already. As Paul puts it a few paragraphs earlier in that same letter, "So, if anyone is in Christ, there is a new creation: everything old has passed away; see, everything has become new!" (2 Corinthians 5:17 NRSV).

Yet even as Paul and his fellow believers received eternal life and entered the new creation, the afflictions of their old lives continued, and the present age with its evils continued also. Therefore, Paul and his fellow believers hoped for the ultimate return of Christ in glory, which he and other New Testament writers refer to as Jesus' "parousia", which means "royal arrival." That is the ultimate hope, which scholars refer to as "future eschatology." Paul's belief in future eschatology stands behind his prayer in 1 Thessalonians 5:23 NRSV: "May the God of peace himself sanctify you entirely; and may your spirit and soul and body be kept sound and blameless at the coming of our Lord Jesus Christ." And it takes expression in his teaching, among other places, in 1 Corinthians 15:24–28 NRSV, where Paul writes,

"Then comes the end, when [Christ] he hands over the kingdom to God the Father, after he has destroyed every ruler and every authority and power. For he must reign until he has put all his enemies under his feet. The last enemy to be destroyed is death. For 'God has put all things in subjection under his feet.' But when it says, 'All things are put in subjection' it is plain that this does not include the one who put all things in subjection under him. When all things are subjected to him, then the Son himself will also be subjected to the one who put all things in subjection under him, so that God may be all in all."

The upshot of Paul's eschatological teaching is that, like Paul, we experience salvation now and, at the same time, hope for its glorious perfection. Like Paul, we know Jesus and experience in part now, and at the same time, we long for the day when we will see Jesus "face to face"—when we will know fully, "even as [we] have been fully known." (1 Corinthians 13:12 NRSV). In the between time, which can be a meantime, we practice the greatest gift of all, which is love. (1 Corinthians 13:13). And to learn love, we turn to Jesus and his kingdom proclamation of the gospel, especially as portrayed in the Synoptic Gospels—Matthew, Mark, and Luke.

# Chapter 3

## The Kingdom (Jesus) Proclamation

"Now after John was arrested, Jesus came to Galilee, proclaiming the good news of God, and saying, "The time is fulfilled, and the kingdom of God has come near; repent, and believe in the good news." (Mark 1:14–15 NRSV).

As I mentioned above, in my various settings for ministry—churches and social agencies, work among students and soldiers, and relations local and global—I felt the need to receive and share a gospel richer than what I knew at the time. As I turned to the Scriptures, I found compelling evidence that the good news of the gospel is more comprehensive than I had realized, and the love of Jesus more inclusive than I had experienced. Paul and the other apostles helped me discover in part the richer gospel for which I searched, and even more help came from Jesus as portrayed in the four Gospels. And I believe that my experience gives you also additional reasons to probe the gospel as far as you can.

One of the incentives for such exploration is that our Lord directly calls all of us to be His witnesses, even to be his ambassadors. We cannot fulfill this charge simply by being sure that our trained pastors and missionaries are doing it. Is it not also the everyday

Christian's responsibility to share their faith? Often I have seen faith deepening as a heart for a larger gospel develops, and I believe we can all deepen our faith as we explore the good news, not only about Jesus but from the words and deeds of our Lord himself. In a summary-introductory passage, the Gospel writer Mark tells us that Jesus "came into Galilee proclaiming the gospel of the Kingdom of God." (Mark 1:14 NRSV). Jesus continued to proclaim and enact the "gospel of the Kingdom" throughout virtually all his public ministry. What was the message of that gospel? We do not find it in so many words, but I believe we can ferret it out. Together we can discover a new perspective on the gospel. We do not want to shrink from the gospel; instead, we want to do justice to the fullness of the good news in the New Testament as a whole. After all, do we not want to do justice to our Lord himself?

Others may choose to look in other directions, but I have strong suspicions that the gospel of the Kingdom, upon which Jesus centered most of his attention during the three and a half years of his public ministry, must especially be looked at afresh. To embark on that fresh look, we can start where all four Gospels begin: the message of John the Baptist.

### The Baptizer and the One Who Is to Come

Most scholars agree that the first Gospel to appear in written form was the Gospel of Mark. Therefore, we do well to note that the opening scene in Mark's Gospel features "John the baptizer [who] appeared in the wilderness." John offered "a baptism of repentance for the forgiveness of sins", (Mark 1:4 NRSV) and he also proclaimed:

> "The one who is more powerful than I is coming after me; I am not worthy to stoop down and untie the thong of his sandals. I have baptized you with water; but he will baptize you with the Holy Spirit." (Mark 1:7–8 NRSV).

The promised baptism with the Holy Spirit seems to begin when John baptizes Jesus. As that baptism takes place, Jesus sees "the heavens torn apart and the Spirit descending like a dove on him." Having received the Spirit, Jesus also hears the voice of his Father in heaven, who says, "You are my Son, the Beloved; with you I am well pleased." (Mark 1:10-11 NRSV). And what are the first words we hear from the Beloved Son of God? Jesus begins his public ministry by stating "the time is fulfilled, *and the kingdom of God has come near*; repent and believe in the good news." (Mark 1:15 NRSV, italics added).

To see the centrality of the kingdom to Jesus' proclamation of the gospel, we can note a few additional passages from the other three written Gospels. In Matthew, John the baptizer signals a new era in the history of salvation when he proclaims, "Repent, for the kingdom of heaven has come near" (Matthew 3:2 NRSV), and when Jesus inaugurates that new era, the first public proclamation from our Lord is the same. "Repent, for the kingdom of heaven has come near." (Matthew 4:17 NRSV). So in Matthew, Jesus repeats John's core message verbatim, with the addition that he not only proclaims the kingdom but also embodies it.

In the Gospel of Luke, the angel Gabriel's birth announcement to Mary includes the message that of her son's "kingdom there will be no end." (Luke 1:33 NRSV). When the adult Jesus began his public ministry, he explained to a crowd surrounding him who before wanted him to stay in their village, "I must proclaim the good news of the kingdom of God to other cities also; for I was sent for this purpose." (Luke 4:43 NRSV). While the kingdom is not as central a theme in the Gospel of John, even there we find Jesus saying to Nicodemus, "Very truly, I tell you, no one can enter the kingdom of God without being born of water and Spirit." (John 3:5 NRSV). In that scene, John complements the message of the Synoptic Gospels. All Gospel writers agree that the gospel is not about a one-time "born again" experience of an individual. Instead, our new birth in Christ leads us and countless others into a whole new world—a new society and even a new creation that the Scriptures call "the kingdom of God." A little more attention to John the baptizer will help us understand, that to experience Jesus bringing the kingdom, we need to receive, from God, eyes to see and ears to hear.


**The Baptizer Asks: Are You the One Who Is to Come?**

When John the baptizer preached the coming of the kingdom by means of the promised Christ (or "Messiah", which means "anointed one"), he seemed to hope that the Anointed King from God would make the world right in a hurry. Preaching to sinful people in a land occupied by a sinful empire, John proclaimed, "Even now the ax is lying at the root of the trees; every tree therefore that does not bear good fruit is cut down and thrown into the fire.". John expected the Messiah to work decisively with a winnowing fork in order "to clear his threshing floor and to gather the wheat into his granary, but the chaff he will burn with unquenchable fire." (Luke 3:9, Luke 3:17 NRSV). But when Jesus began his public ministry, it did not go as John expected.

As John preached truth to power, the ruler known as King Herod objected to John's judgments. According to Luke, on top of "all the evil things that

Herod had done, [he] added to them all by shutting up John in prison." (Luke 3:19–20 NRSV). When John's disciples came to him in prison and reported what Jesus was doing, the Baptizer sent two of his disciples to Jesus to ask, "Are you the one who is to come, or are we to wait for another?" (Luke 7:19 NRSV). In other words, languishing in prison, John asked, "If you are the Messiah, where is the justice that brings messianic peace?"

Jesus responded in the context of healing people from illness and casting out unclean spirits. As he carried out such saving acts, he said to John's disciples, "Go and tell John what you have seen and heard." Jesus then pointed to a series of his actions that fulfilled Isaiah 35 and other Messianic Age prophecies, and he culminated the list with "the poor have good news preached to them. And blessed is anyone who takes no offense at me." (Luke 7:22-23 NRSV).

By means of such a response, Jesus revealed the good news that he was clearing God's threshing floor—overcoming evil—but also he was wielding the ax of righteousness in an unexpected way. Instead of directly attacking sinners, which would eventually include attacking everyone human except himself, Jesus suffered alongside sinners and brought them the power of God in the form of sacrificial love. That sacrificial love included so many "wrong people" that it eventually led both religious and political authorities to work together to crucify Jesus. But within the plan of God, the risen Jesus could explain, "Was it not necessary that the Messiah should suffer these things and then enter into his glory"? (Luke 24:26 NRSV). Rather than coming into the world to condemn sinners, Jesus came to save us, and the power of that suffering love enables us to experience glory in all kinds of conditions, including our own suffering. We can also reach out with sacrificial love to poor people and everyone in need in order to live out the good news of the kingdom that Jesus began with his public ministry, death, and resurrection. And to do that, we can continue to learn from the written Gospels that the crucified and risen Jesus speaks to our everyday situations. By means of telling us parables, Jesus gives us the eyes to see, ears to hear, and hearts to experience his kingdom. So to understand and spread the kingdom, we can turn now to Jesus as a teacher who tells vivid stories.

## Parables of the Kingdom

As Jesus began his public ministry, his earliest actions included continuing in Jewish practices in which he had grown up, and then transforming them creatively. For example, Mark records that after Jesus called his first disciples (Mark 1:16–20), "They went to Capernaum; and when the Sabbath came, he entered the synagogue and taught." (Mark 1:21 NRSV). As Jesus spoke, listeners were astonished by his teachings because "he taught them as one having authority, and not as the scribes." (Mark 1:22 NRSV). By speaking with "authority", Jesus spoke in a way that struck listeners as coming directly from God. And as in the creation account in Genesis 1, so in Jesus' teachings: His words create actions. When Jesus speaks, unclean spirits cry out, people with illnesses receive healing, and lives are changed.

What applies to Jesus' teachings in general applies even more to his parables. When Jesus told these revealing aphorisms or stories, people were led to think in new ways and to take steps toward new lives. Jesus leaves no neutral territory; listeners must either let his words bounce off and harden their indifference to our Lord or they must let his words sink in, take root, and bear fruit. For a vivid example of that action, readers can encounter Jesus through his parable of the sower in Luke 8:4–8. In this brief narrative, which is highly autobiographical, Jesus concluded by portraying his ministry in the form of a farming metaphor by saying to his listeners, "Let anyone with ears to hear listen"! (Luke 8:8 NRSV). As we read the parables, we can pray for such kingdom ears, and like Jesus' first disciples, we can ask our Lord to help us understand "what this parable meant." (Luke 8:9). And as Jesus opens our minds to understand his message, we will find that to us, "it has been given to know the secrets of the kingdom of God." (Luke 8:10 NRSV).


## The Kingdom and the King

Jesus' teachings in general and his parables in particular reveal not only "the secrets of the Kingdom of God" but they reveal the King—Jesus the Messiah. So as we read Jesus' words and ponder his stories, we can experience Jesus as a Teacher, a Royal Ruler, and our Great Physician. (See Matthew's summary of Jesus' ministry in Matthew 4:23—"teaching in synagogues and proclaiming the good news of the kingdom and curing every disease and sickness among the people.") Additionally to encountering Jesus himself in these ways, we can participate in the community that looks to King Jesus as Savior and Lord.

In Matthew 18, Jesus' disciples came to him as Teacher, King, and Healer. When they asked, "Who is the greatest in the kingdom of heaven?", Jesus responded by telling them to humble themselves like children (Matthew 18:1–5 NRSV), radically distance themselves from actions that could lead others to stumble (Matthew 18:6–9), and practice forgiveness in a radical way. When Peter asked Jesus how often a disciple should forgive, Jesus gave a seemingly impossible answer: "Jesus said to [Peter], 'Not seven times, but, I tell you, seventy-seven times" (Matthew 18:22 NRSV)—a biblical number that stands for complete and perfect forgiveness.

In order to prompt his disciples to act on his teachings about forgiveness, Jesus told a frightening parable about an unforgiving servant, whose lack of mercy led him into a place of torture (Matthew 18:33–35). Jesus told such a scary story not to threaten or condemn us but to awaken us to our need to be forgiven and to know him as our Savior. As with all of Jesus' teachings, we will not achieve perfect forgiveness in this life. But in Jesus, we have a perfect Savior who prayed even for those who crucified him and said to God on our behalf, "Father, forgive them; for they do not know what they are doing." (Luke 23:34 NRSV). So as we listen to Jesus' parables and listen in on his prayer from the cross, we find ourselves united not only by our entrance into the kingdom but also by the embrace of our King. As our King, Jesus suffers as a servant, and he opens his arms on the cross so that, as he himself says, "and I, when I am lifted up from earth, will draw all people to myself." (John 12:32 NRSV).

When we study the gospel in the Gospels, we learn how to relate everything in creation to the kingdom of God, and we experience the salvation of the King. We can feel grateful for the Apostle Paul's proclamation of King Jesus crucified and risen, and we can go on to meet Jesus in our everyday lives, which become the setting for eternal life. Through the written Gospels—and especially in the parables—we meet Jesus as a farmer, a cook, a merchant, a fisherman, a parent, and more. And in all these ways, Jesus proclaims, acts out, and incarnates the gospel of the kingdom. May we not say that he "proclaimed" the gospel also by acting it out in the eyes of the people of Israel? And may we not pray for eyes and ears to see and hear him in the world today? Jesus is the person who embodies the gospel; Jesus is the gospel. Amazingly, Jesus entrusts his followers with the call to spread the gospel. So we turn now to gospel communication.


## Kingdom Gospel Communication

As Jesus spread the gospel by sharing his own life in word and deed, he also entrusted this kingdom-bringing message to his disciples. In Mark 1, we see Jesus speaking with such authority that people felt astounded. Having seen and heard how Jesus' words affected unclean spirits, people "kept on asking one another, 'What is this? A new teaching—with authority! He commands even the unclean spirits, and they obey him'." (Mark 1:27 NRSV). So Jesus' words carry objective divine power. As with the Creator in Genesis 1, when Jesus speaks, things happen.

At this same time, Jesus did not rely completely on divine fiat. Instead, he elicited human responses by working with people's faith. For example, when a group of friends brought a man with paralysis to Jesus for healing, Mark recorded that "When Jesus saw their faith, he said to the paralytic, 'Son, your sins are forgiven'." (Mark 2:5 NRSV). Once again, Jesus spoke with such authority that it seems either divine or a blasphemous claim to divinity. Opponents said to themselves, "Why does this fellow speak this way? It is blasphemy! Who can forgive sins but God alone"? (Mark 2:7 NRSV). Instead of overpowering his enemies with sheer power, Jesus appealed to their minds and hearts by questioning them in a thoughtful way and previewing the kingdom with an act of healing. To those open to his presence and message, Jesus evoked a sense of the divine. When the man with paralysis received Jesus' word in a way that empowered him to stand up and walk, people were "amazed and glorified God, saying, 'We have never seen anything like this'"! (Mark 2:12 NRSV).

So the divine and human Jesus interacts with the subjective human side of our dialogue with God by appealing to the faith and sense of wonder in his listeners, and then he honors humanity even further by sharing his authority with people he calls to speak for him. In Matthew 10, Jesus summoned the twelve disciples whom he named as apostles (people sent), and he gave them "authority over unclean spirits, to cast them out, and to cure every disease and every sickness." (Matthew 10:1 NRSV). At this point, the authority of Jesus' followers was more focused on deeds than on teachings. However, after his resurrection, as his direct ministry on earth drew to a close, Jesus called his disciples to share his authority by teaching others what they had learned from him. In this rightly famous Great Commission, Jesus said, "All authority in heaven and on earth has been given to me. Go therefore and make disciples of all nations, baptizing them in the name of the Father and of the Son and of the Holy Spirit, and teaching them to obey everything that I have commanded you. And remember, I am with you always, to the end of the age." (Matthew 28:18–20 NRSV).

As inheritors of that Great Commission, we can ask ourselves, have I received Jesus' teachings as messages that carry the authority of God? Have I shared that message in a way that communicates the presence and respect of God? Jesus reveals what is at stake when people, including ourselves, encounter him when he stated, "Everyone therefore who acknowledges me before others, I also will acknowledge before my Father in heaven; but whoever denies me before others, I also will deny before my Father in heaven." (Matthew 10:32–33 NRSV). And then, only a few sentences later, Jesus extended that encounter when he stated to his disciple-representatives, "Whoever welcomes you welcomes me, and whoever welcomes me welcomes the one who sent me." (Matthew 10:40 NRSV). What an honor and responsibility it is to represent our Lord to our neighbors. In light of that commission, we can seek assurance for ourselves while seeking to spread good news to our neighbors and, thank God, leave the final word to Jesus himself. Just as the Church acknowledges weekly, Jesus Christ "will judge the living and the dead" (Apostles' Creed). Leaving judgment to Jesus is central to the gospel, and it is good news that we can gladly share.

# PART 2
## Additional Gospel Content from the Bible

## Chapter 4

## Genesis and the Human Predicament

"Jesus was about thirty years old when he began his work. He was the son (as was thought) of Joseph, son of Heli ... son of Enos, son of Seth, son of Adam, son of God." (Luke 3:23, 3:38 NRSV).

"For since death came through a human being, the resurrection of the dead has also come through a human being; for as all die in Adam, so all will be made alive in Christ." (1 Corinthians 15:21–22 NRSV).

### The Whole Gospel from the Whole Bible

Having looked at Jesus' own proclamation of the gospel in the Gospels, we can continue to claim a larger gospel by looking at additional material from the Scriptures as a whole. What we call the "Old Testament" was the Bible Jesus read and the story he fulfilled. So to follow Jesus, we can reject literalistic fundamentalism, and at the same time, we can look at biblical books that, according to our Lord himself, are inspired by the Spirit (Mark 12:36) in a way that means "the scripture cannot be annulled" (John 10:35). So to understand the Word who in the beginning "was with God" (John 1:1–2), we can look at the Word as found in the beginning of the Bible—the book of Genesis.

Before turning to Genesis itself, I can pass on some personal reflections and anecdotes that shape my strong feelings about seeing the bonds between Jesus, the gospel, and the Old Testament—especially with respect to what we can call the "human predicament." I state the issue addressed as the "human predicament", that is, a philosophical term that best reflects deep cries of the human soul that only God can answer. Whatever stands in the way of the Divine's answer coming through to human beings becomes a veritable tyrant to the human spirit. The first part of the human predicament is clearly stated at the start of what I can see only as a two-fold apostolic gospel: "...Christ died *for our sins,* and...he was buried...*and that he was raised on the third day...*" (italics added). Especially on the basis of this scripture, a two-fold gospel is explained: It refers to the Cross *and* Resurrection together, often treated together as the apostolic gospel. This clear and concise statement of the good news is ranked very highly by scholars. I have long referred to it in such terms myself. But is not an essential part of this affirmation by Paul disregarded when applied only to human sin and the Cross? In Genesis, the Lord says, "But you must not eat from the tree of the knowledge of good and evil, for when you eat from it *you will certainly die."* (Genesis 2:17 NIV, italics added). Is this not tantamount to declaring that death is the consequence of human sin? And when we turn our minds to death, does not the human predicament as a whole begin to overshadow our thoughts? Surely we need life and light from the gospel of Jesus Christ in order to speak to the whole person and the whole of humanity. I know this truth at both a philosophical and personal level.

Having reflected philosophically, I can pass on some personal observations. One Sunday afternoon during my first pastorate, after phoning me, a gentleman came over to the manse. He, with his family, had visited the church that morning and received a warm welcome from members of the congregation. They were interested in coming again because they were looking for a home church; however, he had one question: "Did I understand you in your sermon today to make some reference to human sin? You don't really believe in human sin, do you?"

I answered him with a number of appropriate passages in the Bible that affirmed the reality and problem of human sin, but they made little impression upon him. He seemed absolutely steeled against the very idea of recognizing sin as anything we have to deal with in our human predicament. At the time, I was unable to get past his issues regarding specific deeds due to my limited vocabulary regarding such challenges. As he left the house, I began to wonder if I had missed an opportunity to approach him for Christ from some other direction. What if we had noted the first occurrence of the word "sin" in the biblical story of Cain and Abel? What if we had then proceeded to explore the conflicts in the family of Abraham and related those conflicts to our own family experiences? Wouldn't that have broadened our understanding of sin and the overall human predicament? And that could have led us to a larger understanding of the gospel as God's response to our plight. By limiting our reading of the Old Testament to a few select passages of our own choosing and then constricting our understanding even of such passages, we miss out on what God would really like to say to us. Even more, we miss out on the fullness of salvation that Jesus offers us.

In a different setting, similar thoughts arose in my mind when a friend raised questions in a more positive manner. In a study session, a friend at an inter-church men's Bible class, which I attended for about three years, asked a provocative question: "Surely all of us need Jesus Christ, but aren't there a variety of ways in which Scripture states the gospel that we trust in, and find appropriate ways of understanding it for ourselves?" After further reflection on that and related questions, I sense that our responsibility also extends to the kind of responses we should encourage on the part of those seriously considering our witness. As I thought about serious listeners, I began to think of the abundance of material that Scripture offers on the gospel, starting with the pre-gospel we have in the Old Testament. The gospel is not always crystal clear to us in its Old Testament presentations, yet at various points in that section of the Scriptures, we can find what scholars and students call theophanies and Christophanies—experiences in which God and Christ appear in striking ways. We can think of Moses at the burning bush and Mount Sinai, and we can recall the children of Israel finding water flowing from a rock (Exodus 3 and 17 respectively). According to the Apostle Paul, "the rock was Christ." (1 Corinthians 10:4). And on the basis of Paul's reflections there and in 2 Corinthians 3, we can expect manifestations of God in Christ when we read the Old Testament.

I hope that my comments regarding Genesis and other Old Testament passages will help readers encounter the God of Abraham, who is also the God and Father of our Lord Jesus Christ. As Paul, quoting from Genesis 15 observes, "Just as Abraham 'believed God, and it was reckoned to him as righteousness'" (Galatians 3:6 NRSV), so can we hear God in the Old Testament in a way that brings faith and right relationships. As Paul also observes, the words in Genesis "were written not for [Abraham's] sake alone, but for ours also." (Romans 4:23–24 NRSV). In my search for biblical foundations for a larger gospel in the Old Testament, I have found more than I expected, and I hope my findings provoke readers to search the Scriptures as part of their efforts to share the larger gospel we can find there.

## Primeval Prologue and Creation-Wide Predicament

In terms of claiming and sharing the larger gospel, we can begin with the beginning. In Genesis 1, we read, "In the beginning when God created the heaven and the earth, the earth was a formless void and darkness covered the face of the deep, while a wind from God swept over the face of the waters." (Genesis 1:1–2 NRSV). Think how often people, communities, and even entire civilizations have experienced life as "a formless void and darkness." Each of us lives through times of disorientation and even chaos, and the same truth applies to the societies in which we live. Consider how it feels when the next verse in the Scriptures actually speaks to our inmost beings: "Then God said, 'Let there be light'; and there was light" (Genesis 1:3). With those words, God gives us illumination and hope, and with them in mind, we can ponder the beginning of the fourth Gospel: "In the beginning was the Word, and the Word was with God, and the Word was God." (John 1:1 NRSV).

As we claim a larger gospel, we read Genesis in dialogue with the Gospel of John, and we interpret all of life in dialogue with the life of Jesus. The larger—we can say simply "biblical"—gospel proclaims that Jesus Christ is not only our personal Savior but also the world's Creator. As "the Word [who] was God" from the beginning, Christ brings light and life into human lives and even enters human life by becoming one of us (John 1:2–3). When we read, "The Word became flesh and lived among us" (John 1:14 NRSV), we can know that Christ both knows our troubles and has the power to see us through them. When we read the Old Testament with all its human drama and pathos, we can enrich our understanding of the New Testament claim that, in Christ, "we do not have a high priest who is unable to sympathize with our weaknesses, but we have one who in every respect has been tested as we are, yet without sin." Therefore, we can read human history and reflect on our own lives while approaching "the throne of grace with boldness, so that we may receive mercy and find grace to help in time of need." (Hebrews 4:15-16 NRSV).

Now, if we wonder to which areas of life the gospel speaks as it fulfills the Old Testament, we can find a lifetime of material in Genesis 1–11, often called the "Primeval Prologue." In these theologically rich chapters, we find God in Christ speaking to issues such as loneliness (Genesis 2:18), marriage and conflicts (Genesis 2:24, 3:16), stress at work (Genesis 3:17), and sibling rivalries or other experiences of jealousy (Genesis 4). God in Christ packs all that and much more into the stories of Eden and Cain and Abel. In the story of Noah and the Flood, the Lord speaks to issues ranging from violence to climate change and creation care, and we can find inspiration and vocation when our Creator-Christ makes a covenant between God "and all flesh that is on the earth." (Genesis 9:17 NRSV). In the story of Babel, our Lord speaks to national and cultural rivalries (Genesis 11:1–9), and knowing such Old Testament stories helps us hear Jesus speaking to the human predicament at the social, political, and even cosmic scale. It is no accident that in order to contend for the true gospel against its initial heresies, the early Church leaders (Church fathers and mothers) insisted—against heretics such as Marcion and the Gnostics)—that the Old Testament is an inspired witness to Christ, and the creation finds renewal in Christ. (See Romans 15 and Revelation 21, among many other passages.)

As an example of such biblical and human thinking, I can pass on the following thoughts on the Genesis account of the origins of the human race, which goes as follows: First, Adam and his wife, Eve, live in harmonious relationship to God, referred to in the Eden story as "the LORD God." (See Genesis 2–3). This representative couple spends their days taking care of Eden, the garden over which God has put them in charge. In doing so, they are in a loving relationship with their Maker, who bent over to breathe life into the nostrils of Adam and formed Eve from Adam's rib, a place that indicates equity. The created and creative pair lives with their Creator, one another, and the world around them in happy harmony. However, because of their sins of disobedience and probably pride as well, God drives them out of the Garden of Eden into a world where, for their survival, they have to struggle with a ground now permeated with resisting "thorns and thistles." For women, the pains of childbirth are increased. Social relationships quickly deteriorate, even within the immediate family, as in the Cain and Abel conflict. Such biblical scenes reflect human scenes throughout history and into our own lives.

Coupled with separation from God, humankind has been struggling with the imperfect, even groaning, world for which they are still responsible. (See Romans 8:18–25.) The original couple and their descendants find themselves enmeshed with an environment starkly different from Eden and beyond the reach of their own ability to restore—all this on top of the corrupting impact of human sin. A change in the natural, social, and work environments, which Adam, Eve, and their successors have to deal with, follows from the corrupting effects of human sin. As they had been warned ahead of time in their call to obedience to God, their failure to obey does indeed lead directly to death. As they realize the consequences of their actions, they experience death in relationships, and they know that they will someday die physically. As those who live in that world which we have inherited, we can find truth and hope by reading Genesis in communion with Christ.

Another truth that emerges from such reading is that in the early chapters of Genesis, the two-sided character of the natural world is stated, and the same complexity of our social world may also be inferred. Regarding the first humans, Genesis states, "God blessed them, and God said to them, 'Be fruitful and multiply, and fill the earth and subdue it; and have dominion over the fish of the sea and over the birds of the air and over every living thing that moves upon the earth.'" (Genesis 1:28 NRSV). These words, I believe, make up what we may call God's early assignment to the human race. This "cultural mandate", so to speak, includes God giving us responsibility to exercise stewardship over his living creation. It also includes the sad story in which one brother takes the life of another, and when confronted by God, he gives the irresponsible answer, "am I my brother's keeper"? (Genesis 4:9 NRSV). Yet the early assignment remains and, surprisingly to some, has been carried out to a remarkable extent in more modern times via the agricultural revolution, the industrial revolution, the cosmic revolution, and today's communication revolution (which has not run its full course). We can well see today how no single human family or tribe could possibly, in developing the potential of the earth, take custody, explore, and so take charge of God's earth. In all three areas, we have had developments that only God could foresee, but side by side with the good grain of God's experiment, there has been a development of evil. In no place is this mixture of good and evil more pronounced than in the impact of the "world" upon human life.

As these extensions of the human predicament became evident to the first couple, the words of their first deceiver must also have occurred to them. The prospect of possibly being forced to continue to deal with his deceptive influences must have begun to dawn upon their consciences and become manifest in their changed natural world and a changed social environment. No longer was it possible to think of the human predicament in terms of a single tyrannical reality facing both Adam and those who would follow, because of his yielding to the tempter's pressure to doubt God's warning about the tree by which he would know evil by doing evil. The inward corruption of sin coupled with its consequence in the termination of his existence as he then knew it must have been utterly frightful. His world to which he was assigned such far-reaching responsibility became a far more difficult world to subdue or have dominion over.

In addition to the dire inward realities of sin and death, Adam would have to also face external forces of an evil spiritual power that had lured him into conscious disobedience to God with the words "You will not die" (Genesis 3:4 NRSV). To sin had been added the further element of his own death. Yet still further, Adam and the race that followed him (which, in some sense, he seemed to represent) would also have to deal with deceptions and temptations from the same satanic powers all their days. And with a troublesome, at times ravaging, natural world and a social world outside of them, we can recall one of Paul's brief summaries regarding the human predicament: "without were fightings [the world and Satan], within were fears [sin and death]", (2 Corinthians 7:5 KJV). We can rejoice with Paul that thanks to God in Christ, we can have confidence in God and one another "in all things." (2 Corinthians 7:16 KJV).

## Illumination from Aulén: Three Tyrants—and More?

To live wisely in the world while seeking communion and confidence in God, we can find illumination from a Swedish theologian named Gustaf Aulén (1879–1977). He contributes strongly to our quest to find a larger gospel.

Less than a century ago came the stunning claim by Gustaf Aulén that the central meaning of Jesus' death was his victory over an array of evil powers—"Tyrants", as he called them. I consider this designation of the Swedish theologian's so apt that I will often make use of the word "tyrant" to refer to external evils from this point on.

In Christianity's first thousand years, Aulén saw what we can call the "Christus Victor" theory as the prevailing "theory of the atonement." Other main atonement theories come to us under the titles of "ransom theory", "vicarious (or substitutionary) atonement", and "imitation of Christ." Aulén appears to stake his major argument upon the historical theology of the early church fathers, stemming particularly from Irenaeus. Whether readers concur that Aulén's "ransom theory of the atonement" dominated the first half of Christianity's history or whether they see it as just one important theory of that period, we can certainly agree that his historical argument is suggestive for comprehending the extent of the human predicament as well as God's corresponding redemptive action.

In addition to Tyrant Sin, Aulén recognizes two other deadly tyrants: Death, a consequence of Sin, and the objective spiritual powers of Evil, which are hinted at in Genesis and later given further revelation in passages such as Ephesians 6:10–20. But from the perspective taken in this book, Aulén's historical argument by itself cannot be decisive. Neither can the wide range of human needs reflected in Scripture in themselves be decisive. We must, then, in a theocentric gospel, go on to ask whether there are scriptural grounds for understanding God's critical redemptive acts through Jesus Christ. I must agree with Aulén that facing Death represents one of the most searching issues of our human spirit. I personally find his view reassuring that the gospel addresses our human mortality in addition to sin.

Aulén further refers to a nefarious, objective, and personal spiritual power, variously called "the devil", "Satan", "Lucifer", or "prince of this world." Other such forces associated with the evil one and subservient to him and his purposes are "demons" and angels that have sinned. (See 2 Peter 2:4.) Jesus certainly operates with these categories of reality, as we see in his temptation conflicts and in his description of the work of his followers. (See Luke 4:1–13 and 10:1–20.) The significance of Jesus seeing "Satan fall from heaven like a flash of lighting" (Luke 10:18 NRSV) would seem to be that heaven can be regarded not only as a future destination but even more as a present reality that is present everywhere. We can see heaven as God's special and sacred abode, as near to us as the atmosphere that surrounds us, and we can feel grateful that Satan and his allies were removed from the company of other angelic beings. (See Revelation 12 for a dramatic portrait of this unseen but real spiritual realm.)

For many people today, the idea of a personal devil is the furthest thing from their minds. In light of a biblical description of Satan, whether in the "Fall of Adam" or with respect to the demons that had possessed or taken control of human lives until they were exorcised by Jesus in his Galilean ministry, I can imagine personal devils saying, "Such skepticism and inattention are just fine with me." As C.S. Lewis notes in *The Screwtape Letters*, demons like nothing more than to be disbelieved in. Others view the scriptural description of Satan as one embodying objective, spiritual powers of evil. They maintain that it is an example of the conveyance of revealed truth in Scripture through metaphorical language. As with some other metaphorical or suspected metaphorical language, is a clear resolution of this question an absolutely crucial matter? In my view, the answer is no. I believe there are many who view the "evil powers" as other than those of a personal devil with a cohort of personal demons, but they do view them as real, objective powers of evil.

As I operate from my partial but vital perspective, I see a correspondence between the way particular kinds of human sin work and the presence of spiritual powers in everyday life. It seems to be a phenomenon that occurs periodically throughout history, where certain human lives are utterly possessed by demonic power. There may be also isolated, hurtful acts attributed to the devil. A biblical illustration has the enemy referred to by Jesus in a parable recorded in Matthew 13:24–30. There Jesus says, "The kingdom of heaven may be compared to someone who sowed good seed in his field; but while everybody was asleep, an enemy came and sowed weeds among the wheat, and then went away." Whether or not an individual regards the devil as a literal power of evil endowed with personhood, or as a mistaken human personification of a sinister reality, is less important. What is important is if a person simply dismisses the biblical concept from one's understanding of the human predicament. For myself, I have no problem recognizing here a scriptural allusion to the devil as a literal, personal being. I find it helps me to understand an undesirable element in the human predicament, and it is an especially potent element of evil because it is endowed with personhood.

We can gain additional insight when we note the Gospel account that concludes, "When the devil had finished every test, he departed from him until an opportune time." (Luke 4:13 NRSV). From this account, with some justification, we may conclude that the devil works systematically upon us within the areas of weakness that he wants to test. The key is to recognize and to resist the temptations that are at hand, and with confidence that with resistance on our part there will come, at least for a time, relief from those temptations. But as with other problems of the human predicament, we should not depend just on ourselves. First of all, we must depend on Christ himself for forgiveness from the sin of our disobedience and pride and, second, the inherent consequence of sin—death, both physical and spiritual.

The Bible deals with personified evil in the context of the perfect Personhood of God and the personhood of our humanity, as created in God's image. Therefore, is it altogether surprising that the most far-reaching challenge to God and humanity should come from evil embodied in perverted personhood? But where distinguishing metaphorical language is of prominent concern, I hesitate to regard as imperative an "either/or" solution that very often is, to an important degree, a matter of intellectual perception. However, if the language does not evidence recognition of a host of evil powers opposing God and humankind, but in effect explains them away, it cannot be accepted as representing the biblical view of the four evangelists or the Apostle Paul.

In now broadly recognized social issues such as ethnic discrimination, injustices to women, and exploitation of those in society who have been unable to defend themselves, society has often had to reach outside of biblical revelation to God's general revelation of his law written on the hearts of humankind, the universal sense of right and wrong, in order to seek and, in part, achieve social justice. (See Romans 2:15 and Hebrews 10:16.) How better to account for such moral obtuseness than that one rooted in the Scriptures, which presents the evil one to us as having unusual skills coupled with the most devious of motivations? Consequently, such evil actions have to be viewed as among the most sinister and challenging realities that we can experience. The sad alternative of insensitivity to sin and evil is not only morally inexcusable to fellow believers and the human family; it is an offense to Christ himself. As Jesus puts it in one his most alarming parables, "Truly I tell you, just as you did not do it to one of the least of these, you did not do it to me." (Matthew 25:45 NRSV).

The issue of spiritual forces of evil also sheds light on numerous ethical issues, especially social justice, sometimes even ahead of the Christian community itself. One of these was the social injustice of human slavery, where Renaissance thinking on that issue appeared to move ahead faster than the general Christian witness, at least in some parts of our own country. I like the term "general revelation" for this phenomenon, but I feel that Roman Catholic thought expresses it in a more forthright manner through references to "natural law."

Although we are called to resist sin wherever it occurs, is it amiss that we need special warnings against such oversights? Do we not also need redemption from what brings such far-reaching damages into human life? This is represented to us in Scripture as the quiet but devious ways by which the serpent can slither his way into our decisions and actions, sometimes even while we imagine we are being obedient to God. How threatening to the human soul such battles can be! Where else can we hope to turn, other than to Christ, for power that has the capacity to defeat such deadly threats? As 2 Corinthians 4:4 applies to Satan's work in blinding our eyes to the gospel, is there any form of the gospel to which this applies more than to the power of Christ's redemption over the power of Satan?

An important scripture reads, "There is no longer Jew or Greek, there is no longer slave or free, there is no longer male and female; for all of you are one in Christ Jesus." (Galatians 3:28 NRSV). This principle ought to be compelling for all who belong to Christ. But can we think that this scripture bothered the evil one throughout the centuries? Nonetheless, this scriptural truth was met with little resistance by Christians to slavery and sexism in our world. Whether by Christians or others, might it have been misunderstood because of Satan's influence on us, giving false meaning and only serving as a salve to our conscience? It is our failing, being so dilatory in taking the responsible action in regard to relationships in which God calls us, to implement what we see in Scripture.

A figure of the devil, strikingly in contrast with that of a serpent, meets us in 1 Peter 5:8 NRSV. There we read that "like a roaring lion your adversary the devil prowls around, looking for someone to devour." Only the powers attributed to Satan in the Scriptures can account for the vast deception of a governmental regime—"German National Socialism" under Hitler—dedicated to evil so far-reaching that many people of good faith simply could not believe, until it was too late to resist effectively, that evil on such a scale was happening around them. Or that the government—any government—was so protected by Romans 13:1 that it had to be obeyed in its own realm under any conditions whatever. It is shocking and humbling that the entire continent in which Christianity blossomed into what came to be called "Christendom" could easily, for decades or more, become subservient to a government skilled in the institutionalization of evil. Here the work of the devil was very different from the quiet subtleties of serpentine satanic action, and yet it is perhaps history's most flagrant example of the work of Satan as the roaring lion.

Furthermore, the unappealing yet unavoidable theme of institutionalized evil connects with the Cross itself. Jesus mentions the instigator of this special kind of deception. This is his decisive, though not yet final, victory over Satan. As the hour of his death drew near, Jesus stated, "Now is the judgment of this world; now

93

the ruler of this world will be driven out." (John 12:31 NRSV). The term "ruler" suggests both the widespread and deep influence of Satan over the world in which we live. For readers inclined to take little thought for what Scripture says about Satan, a review of C. S. Lewis' classic work, *The Screwtape Letters*, could be illuminating and at the same time utterly delightful reading.

Having recognized as tyrants Sin, Death, and the Devil, it would seem but a small step to add to Aulén's list the tyrannical impact that "the world" has on our humanity. Along with dealing with the demonic powers, "the world" constituted another major concern of Jesus' early ministry in Galilee, with its focus on "the gospel of the Kingdom of God." I, therefore, call attention to yet a fourth principal category of the human predicament— the ravages of the world. Both the activity of Satan and the nature of life in this world are tyrants to the human spirit from the outside. With respect to "the world", we can ask: How often do we find this complexity in the human life we experience? Some events, the effects of which at first appear to be a great opportunity or blessing, turn out to be a disaster or the other way around. Biblical teachings regarding "the world" do not answer every question when such events arise, but they do stimulate us to think and act with increased insight.

In light of the importance and complexity of the phrase "the world", we can note that the term is troublesome unless we notice distinctions in its biblical usage. Even after the fall of Adam and its consequent curse upon the world in Adam's charge, the Scriptures also frequently refer to the world favorably as a source of God's ongoing blessing to us. Rain and sunshine fall on the just and unjust alike. The skies proclaim God's handiwork and his glory (Psalm 19). These and many other Old Testament passages speak to us in a similar vein. Building on that theme, in Romans 1:20, Paul declares, "Ever since the creation of the world [God's] eternal power and divine nature, invisible though they are, have been understood and seen through the things he has made." All such blessings of the world around us, in nature and in human life, can attract us or be misused, not just those specifically mentioned by Jesus in his gospel of the Kingdom of God. So often we are caught up by the blessing at the expense of the "Blesser." The good things of life as well as the bad can tempt us and hurt us by becoming idols or being put ahead of God. Scripture further employs the term "the world", which God loved even "while we still were sinners" (Romans 5:8), and it is in this sense that he likely referred to it in John 3:16 as the world God so loved that he gave his only Son. In light of such love, which can be deflected by idolatry, we must resolve not to get carried away and make good things into false gods.

These various themes encourage future reflection on the human predicament and God's response to our plight. We can note that the curse that humankind brought upon itself extended also to the created world that God, in the early assignment, entrusted to human custody, (Note both Genesis 1:28 and Genesis 3:22–24) and brought these two creation accounts into dialogue with Christ. Where Paul declares, "... in Christ God was reconciling the world to himself" (2 Corinthians 5:19), Aulén sees a reconciliation between God and the entire creation, both natural and human. It is a statement on which he places considerable emphasis, and it calls us to creative thinking and a wide application of the larger gospel. As a beginning observation, we can note that sin, or sometimes the powers of both Sin and Death, are addressed in what we know as the apostolic gospel or as the Cross and Resurrection. The tyranny of Satan and the ravages of the world are addressed in the gospel of the Kingdom of God, as declared by Jesus in Galilee and also by the Apostolic Gospel as preached by Paul. We who seek the larger gospel of the entire Scriptures and also general revelation can ponder and act on all these themes.

At a practical level, we can observe that a major part of Jesus' ministry in Galilee was his effort to deliver the Israelite people from a wide and desperate range of concrete human predicaments: bodily illnesses and disabilities, physical dangers such as storms on the Sea of Galilee, and conditions such as hunger and poverty, which Jesus addressed in nature miracles, including food for a hungry multitude that had been listening to his teaching for much of the day, those enduring false charges and persecution for his sake, and many more. In another example of how the Kingdom Gospel and Apostolic Gospel complement one another, we can note that Paul conceptualizes for us these and other such disastrous examples of the human condition in the expression, "this present evil world." (Galatians 1:4 KJV). To overcome that world and to bring in a different world, a new creation that includes the age of messianic peace and joy, Jesus "gave himself" for our sins (Galatians 1:4). With that sacrifice, Jesus liberated us from sin and evil at both the most personal and the most cosmic levels. So we can join Paul in saying to Jesus and God the Father, "...glory forever and ever. Amen." (Galatians 1:5 NRSV). When the ravages of the fallen world threaten to overwhelm us and when we see how cruel the world can be, we can gain strength to overcome by the larger gospel of Jesus Christ.

## Expansion of Aulén via Ladd

Having passed on biblical reflections related to the writings of Gustaf Aulén, I can mention another biblical theologian who has had a major impact on me in my quest for a larger gospel. I refer here to George Eldon Ladd, who for many years served as Professor of New Testament at Fuller Theological Seminary in

Pasadena, California. One area in which I learned much from Ladd has to do with biblical eschatology. (For more on that topic, you may turn to Chapter 9 and read about Ladd in the subsection called "Excellent Example".) Another area in which I learned from Ladd and which I will explore here has to do with healing. The key point to ponder here is that Jesus' victory over forces of evil can take the form of healings, and the further point is that victories in the form of healings point to Jesus overcoming all injustice and bringing healing to the human predicament as a whole.

A central passage to guide us here appears in Luke 7:18–35. (See also the parallel passage in Matthew 11:2–9.) By this time in Luke's Gospel, Jesus had been carrying out his public ministry in ways that have brought him wide recognition. Luke tells us that as Jesus carried out his work in Galilee "a report about him spread through all the surrounding country" (Luke 4:14 NRSV). Jesus experienced both praise and rejection, and that mixed response, along with the unexpected character of Jesus' actions, had left John the Baptist perplexed. Therefore, from a prison in which he had been shut up by Herod (see Luke 3:18–20), John sent two disciples to ask Jesus, "Are you the one who is to come, or are we to wait for another?" (Luke 7:19 NRSV).

Gospel readers can certainly understand why John sent this challenging question to Jesus. Having rejoiced in the coming of Jesus while still in his mother's womb (Luke 1:41), John had made preaching about the coming of the longed-for Messiah central to his dynamic public ministry. To crowds of people needing repentance and direction, John warned that the Lord would soon overcome evil with dramatic actions, which he compared to the power of an ax "lying at the root of the trees" (Luke 3:9). John expected the Lord to defeat evil swiftly and to bring the fruit of a just society in a clearly visible way. John anticipated a day in which evildoers would be treated like bad trees about to be "cut down and thrown into the fire" (Luke 3:9), and that social salvation would happen by the powerful actions of the Messiah, which John summed up by saying:

> "I baptize you with water; but one who is more powerful than I is coming; I am not worthy to untie the thong of his sandals. He will baptize you with the Holy Spirit and fire. His winnowing fork is in his hand, to clear his threshing floor and to gather the wheat into his granary, but the chaff he will burn with unquenchable fire." (Luke 3:16–17).

In addition to preparing the way for Jesus with such strong words, John also baptized Jesus with an action in which "the heaven was opened" (Luke 3:21), so we can understand why John expected a rapid and complete overcoming of the evil one. As the Messiah, filled with the Holy Spirit, Jesus seemed poised to fulfill immediately the words of John's father, Zechariah, who had prophesied about "a mighty savior", who would save God's people from their "enemies and from the hand of all who hate us" (Luke 1:69, 71). Yet now, as John languished in prison due to a travesty of justice, what was Jesus doing? He was certainly not eradicating all evildoers. Nor was he liberating oppressed people like John from their prisons.

In a revealing way, Jesus responded to John's question first by curing "many people of diseases" (Luke 7:21). The point to see here and elsewhere is that Jesus' healing ministry includes wider actions than physical cures. Jesus' healing ministry includes overcoming entire plagues and casting out evil spirits (Luke 7:21). After such broadly healing actions, Jesus put his saving work into words by saying:

> "Go and tell John what you have seen and heard: the blind receive their sight, the lame walk, the lepers are cleansed, the deaf hear, the dead are raised, the poor have good news brought to them. And blessed is anyone who takes no offense at me." (Luke 7:22–23 NRSV).

Jesus blessed those who took no offense to him because he knew that, like John, all his followers would feel surprised at his way of overcoming evil not primarily with actions of punishment but, instead, with goodness in the form of humility and healing (cf. Romans 12:21)—a healing way that we can call "the way of the cross." In the Gospel of Luke, Jesus' way of the cross began with his humble birth narrative. After sending his angel Gabriel to announce the birth of the child who would become John the Baptist to a barren old couple (See Luke 1:5–25), God went on to make a birth announcement to a lowly young maiden named Mary. (See Luke 1:26–38.) Mary, who saw herself as living in a state of "lowliness" (Luke 1:48), celebrated the coming of her child by praising God for the way in which

> "He has shown strength with his arm; he has scattered the proud in the thoughts of their hearts. He has brought down the powerful from their thrones, and lifted up the lowly"; (Luke 1:51–52 NRSV)

That humble yet powerful way of overcoming injustice continued when, as a newborn, Jesus rested in a manger, which previews his death on a cross. (See Luke 2 and 23). This continued as the adult Jesus made his final preparation for his public ministry on Earth by being "led by the Spirit in the wilderness, where for forty days he was tempted by the devil." (Luke 4:1–2 NRSV). The point to see in this spiritual battle is that the devil tempted Jesus in terms of worldly power, but Jesus responded with humble obedience. (See Luke 4:1–13).

According to Luke, after tempting Jesus in the wilderness three times, the devil "departed from him until an opportune time." (Luke 4:13). That opportune time came in the garden of Gethsemane. In that place, Jesus prays to be spared, if possible, not only from the physical torture of the cross but even more from the ultimate attack of the evil one. Jesus' Father in heaven heard his Son's prayer and sent an angel from heaven to appear to Jesus and to give "him strength" (Luke 22:43). That strength took the form of Jesus praying so earnestly that "his sweat became like great drops of blood falling on the ground." (Luke 22:44 NRSV). Such godly strength was not visible to people thinking only in worldly terms, but it sustained Jesus in the arrest that led to his crucifixion. When his opponents, armed with swords and clubs, arrested him, Jesus responded courageously by saying, "When I was with you day after day in the temple, you did not lay hands on me. But this is your hour, and the power of darkness!" (Luke 22:53 NRSV).

Jesus endured the hour of injustice that led to the darkness of the cross, and that turned out to be God's way of defeating the evil one. Jesus prayed for forgiveness for those who crucified him (Luke 23:34), and opened paradise to a true criminal who asked for his kingdom. (Luke 23:42–43). Jesus entrusted his spirit into the hands of his Father (Luke 23:46), and his Father in heaven responded by raising him from the dead and sitting him at his right hand. (Luke 22:69). What Luke and the other Gospel writers portray in narrative form, the Apostle Paul expresses in hymn-like form in several passages from his Epistles. As Paul puts it in Colossians 1:19–20, in Christ "all the fullness of God was pleased to dwell, and through him God was pleased to reconcile to himself all things, whether on earth or in heaven, by making peace through the blood of the cross." (For related "powers" passages, see Romans 8:38, 1 Corinthians 15:24, and Ephesians 1:21).

Jesus' victory through the blood of the cross reveals that he and his Father act with the power of the Holy Spirit not to punish and destroy humanity but instead to heal and save the human family. As the Son of God, Jesus came "to destroy the works of the devil" (1 John 3:8), and that meant loving the world God made. (John 3:16). During Jesus' ministry on Earth, that healing, saving power came in the form of healing illnesses and liberating spirits. In his major work, *A Theology of the New Testament,* Ladd sums up these related actions of Jesus in a helpful way. In a chapter called "The Need of the Kingdom", Ladd devotes pages to Jesus' spiritual victory in subsections such as "The Spirit-World", "Satan", and "Demons" (pp. 45–56). Then, in a chapter called "The New Age of Salvation", Ladd demonstrates that the "presence of the messianic salvation is also seen in Jesus' miracles of healing." (p.76). Ladd argues rightly that when Jesus heals bleeding, blindness, possession, and even death itself, this reveals God's concern not only with souls but with the whole of human persons. This strong and wide healing salvation brings joy in heaven and on earth and its fullness in bringing both physical healing and wider salvation. Luke's story of the lepers reveals this truth. Jesus marvelously heals ten lepers of their illness, and then only one of the ten returns to Jesus to offer thanksgiving. According to Luke, the story concludes as follows:

> "He prostrated himself at Jesus' feet and thanked him. And he was a Samaritan. Then Jesus asked, 'Were not ten made clean? But the other nine, where are they? Was none of them found to return and give praise to God except this foreigner?' Then he said to him, 'Get up and go on your way; your faith has made you well.'" (Luke 17:11-19 NRSV).

In the original Greek, the words translated "your faith has made you well" can also be translated as "your faith has saved you." Ponder the breadth of Jesus' salvation. It includes curing an illness, which leads to thankful worship and which points to unity between divided groups such as Jews and Samaritans—all of which expresses our Lord's victory over the evil one. In a world that needs healing in every way, we need such a Savior, and that is who our Father has given us in Jesus Christ. So how do we participate more fully in such a gospel and such a salvation? We realize that we can come to Jesus as our Great Physician. In his Gospel, Luke, also known as the beloved physician, portrays Jesus healing a paralyzed man by forgiving his sins and then healing a compromised man by calling him to discipleship. (See Luke 5:17–32). When some of his adversaries questioned why Jesus showed such healing love to sinners, Jesus answered by stating, "Those who are well have no need of a physician, but those who are sick; I have come to call not the righteous but sinners to repentance." (Luke 5:31–32 NRSV). No wonder Jesus' followers have for centuries agreed that confession is good for the soul. Knowing our need for a Savior leads us to Jesus, to his healing, and to an ever-expanding gospel. In the words of a title from an important book by George Eldon Ladd, when we receive such healing and respond to such a gospel, we experience *The Presence of the Future.*

# Chapter Five

# Isaiah and Prophetic Vision

"For whatever was written in former days was written for our instruction, so that by steadfastness and by the encouragement of the scriptures we might have hope. May the God of steadfastness and encouragement grant you to live in harmony with one another, in accordance with Christ Jesus, so that together you may with one voice glorify the God and Father of our Lord Jesus Christ." (Romans 15:4–6 NRSV).

## Motifs and Motivations

During my years as a student at Union Theological Seminary, I met a teacher who made the Scriptures in their fullness come alive for me in a fresh way. Dr. Josef Hromádka gave a series of lectures at Union right after his arrival as a refugee from communist Czechoslovakia. Perhaps his experiences with tyranny and escape gave him a better feel for biblical themes such as exodus and exile. In any case, his talks intrigued me, and he became my major professor in my doctoral studies at Princeton Theological Seminary during the ensuing years. He helped me experience Paul's claim that what we call the Old Testament "was written in former days for our instruction." (Romans 15:4).

One powerful element in Dr. Hromádka's teaching was that rather than speaking about "themes" in the Scriptures, he referred regularly to scriptural "motifs." The way he presented those motifs gave me a feel for the distinctive driving power of the Word and the way in which the Spirit moves it into the human heart. His perceptive theological thinking, especially when he incorporated both Calvin and Luther, was accompanied by a warm friendliness of spirit, whether in the classroom or at the many student gatherings in his home. I trust that his spirit, as well as the Holy Spirit, can help us encounter both the blazing holiness and the warm love of God as we continue to allow the Old Testament to enlarge our understanding and practice of the gospel.

**The Promised King**

When our Lord Jesus preached his gospel of the kingdom, he spoke as one Jew to his fellow Jews. And when Paul preached his Apostolic gospel, he preached "to the Jew first and also to the Greek." (Romans 1:16). It follows that the gospel, especially as first given to the Jewish community, reflects a great deal of Old Testament thought in general. It also reflects Israel's religious practices of the ceremonial and moral law. And its national history under its kings prepared the way for an ideal king, a coming Messiah king. For us to understand the gospel of Jesus Christ and how it both fulfilled the hopes of and surprised the Jewish people, we do well to trace biblical hopes for the promised "anointed one", which is the English translation of the Hebrew word "messiah" and the Greek word "Christ."

Jewish hopes for an ideal king go back to early and difficult times in the history of Israel. During the days of the judges, Israel lacked consistent leadership and a unifying vision. With a refrain that occurs several times in the final chapter of the book of Judges, the author depicts a nation on the brink of self-destruction and, with sad realism, observes, "In those days there was no king in Israel; all the people did what was right in their own eyes." (Judges 21:25 NRSV).

In the book of Samuel (which has been canonized as First Samuel and Second Samuel), the biblical author depicts leaderless Israel also threatened by external enemies—primarily a group called the Philistines. During this time of national distress, the Israelite woman Hannah also felt personal anguish because she "had no children." (Samuel 1:2). In the ancient world, infertility carried a social stigma, and Hannah's shame was compounded by the mockery of her husband's other wife, Peninnah. Peninnah "used to provoke [Hannah] severely" (1 Samuel 1:6), so Hannah prayed fervently for the Lord to open her womb. When she received her first child, Samuel, Hannah celebrated with a prayer that foreshadows Mary's "Magnificat" (prayer of praise) in relation to the birth of Jesus. (See Luke 1:46–55). Hannah's prayer includes not only praise for God ending her barren status but it also looks forward to the day when the Lord "will give strength to his king, and exalt the power of his anointed." (1 Samuel 2:10 NRSV).

As noted above, the word "anointed" translates into English the Hebrew word "Messiah" and the Greek word "Christ", so Hannah's prayer regarding Samuel also previews Simeon's celebration of the child Jesus as the royal savior of the world. When the Spirit led Simeon to pray for Joseph and Mary's son, the infant Jesus, Simeon could say to God, "...for my eyes have seen your salvation, which you have prepared in the presence of all peoples, a light for revelation to the Gentiles, and for glory to your people Israel." (Luke 2:30–32 NRSV).

The birth, life, and ministry of Samuel led first to the anointing of Saul, Israel's first but failed king, and then to the anointing of David. King David had infamous flaws, but his courage as a warrior, his skills as a musician, and even his passion as a dancer (2 Samuel 6) led the nation of Israel and later the Jewish people to look to God to send them a king even greater than David. One passage that expresses that hope, not only for Israel but also for the whole earth, comes in Psalm 72. This messianic hope—this hope for an anointed king whose rule reflects the reign of God—expresses biblical hope so eloquently that it is worth quoting in full. If offers what we could call a truly biblical prosperity gospel because it is a prosperity that includes justice for the poor. The vision goes as follows:

> "Give the king your justice, O God, and your righteousness to a king's son. May he judge your people with righteousness, and your poor with justice. May the mountains yield prosperity for the people, and the hills, in righteousness. May he defend the cause of the poor of the people, give deliverance to the needy, and crush the oppressor.
>
> May he live while the sun endures, and as long as the moon, throughout all generations. May he be like rain that falls on the mown grass, like showers that water the earth. In his days may righteousness flourish and peace abound, until the moon is no more.
>
> May he have dominion from sea to sea, and from the River to the ends of the earth. May his foes bow down before him, and his enemies lick the dust. May the kings of Tarshish and of the isles render him tribute, may the kings of Sheba and Seba bring gifts. May all kings fall down before him, all nations give him service.

*For he delivers the needy when they call,
the poor and those who have no helper.
He has pity on the weak and the needy,
and saves the lives of the needy. From
oppression and violence he redeems
their life; and precious is their blood in
his sight.*

*Long may he live! May gold of Sheba be
given to him. May prayer be made for
him continually, and blessings invoked
for him all day long. May there be
abundance of grain in the land; may it
wave on the tops of the mountains; may
its fruit be like Lebanon; and may people
blossom in the cities like the grass of the
field. May his name endure forever, his
fame continue as long as the sun. May
all nations be blessed in him; may they
pronounce him happy.*

*Blessed be the L*ORD*, the God of Israel,
who alone does wondrous things.
Blessed be his glorious name forever;
may his glory fill the whole earth. Amen
and Amen."*
*(Psalm 72 NRSV)*

Now even a cursory knowledge of Israel's history
as recorded in the Scriptures lets us know that neither
David's son Solomon nor any of David's royal
descendants lived up to the hope of Psalm 72 until the
birth of Jesus. As the psalmist and other biblical writers

hoped, Jesus was able to incarnate a glory that fills the whole earth but only because he fulfilled biblical promises in an unexpected, almost unimaginable, way. And that leads us to the next section in our chapter: the anointed king as suffering servant.

## Unexpected Exaltation of Suffering Servant

When we have Psalm 72 and other passages of messianic hope in mind, the prophet Isaiah's vision of the idea to come becomes the more striking. The book of Isaiah helps us claim a larger gospel in several ways. For example, as we trace God's promises in Isaiah—and especially in relation to Isaiah 52,53 - we will find the gospel speaking not only in terms of an anointed one bearing our sins but also a servant who brings healing to a whole range of human sorrows. Just a few passages from the majestic book of Isaiah will illustrate that width of a great salvation as presented in a larger gospel.

In chapter 7 of the book that will, in time, be named for him, the prophet Isaiah speaks to King Ahaz. The year is approximately 735 BC, so Israel has been divided into the northern kingdom of Israel and the southern kingdom of Judah for about two centuries. The descendants of David rule the southern kingdom of Judah, and the current Davidic monarch, Ahaz, faces attacks from the nearby country of Syria as well as the northern kingdom of Israel, also referred to as

"Ephraim." As Ahaz and his people shake with fear "as the trees of the forest shake before the wind" (Isaiah 7:2), Isaiah comes with a powerful promise from the Lord. Through his prophet, the Lord promises that his people will withstand the attack, so the prophet calls the king to "stand firm in faith." (Isaiah 7:9). In response to Ahaz's lack of faith, the Lord promises a child to be born, who will be named Immanuel, which means, "God with us."

When Christians read Isaiah 7:14, which promises a child to be born to a "young woman" in the Hebrew Scriptures, or a "virgin" in the Greek translation of the Old Testament called the Septuagint, our thoughts go immediately to the birth of Jesus as recorded in Matthew 1:18–25, which includes a quotation from Isaiah 7:14. To see and celebrate that fulfillment is right and proper for Christians as long as we do not forget the earthly and political setting in which Isaiah spoke the promise to Ahaz. Like Isaiah and Ahaz, Joseph and Mary, and our friends and enemies in every time and place, we live in a world of national conflicts and the rise and fall of great powers. So when our gospel and our faith expand to include a vision of the Lord ruling even during times that seem frightening, we can expand our lives to include earthly and political practices that follow from a biblically expanded faith. For example, during times of polarization, we can seek what it means to live out the teachings of the Son of

God, who says, "Blessed are the peacemakers, for they will be called children of God." (Matthew 5:9 NRSV). Can we actually seek peace on Earth in the real world? We can when we know Jesus as Immanuel, God with us, as he is revealed in both Isaiah 7 and Matthew 1. And similar observations and applications apply to other messianic passages in the magisterial book of Isaiah.

To give just a couple of examples, we can look at the promise of an ideal king given in Isaiah 9. Once again, many Christians will find the passage familiar, especially if we attend worship during Advent and on Christmas. Through his prophet Isaiah, the Lord promises a royal child who will be named "...Wonderful Counselor, Mighty God, Everlasting Father, Prince of Peace." (Isaiah 9:6 NRSV). When we think of Isaiah proclaiming this hope during the troubled times of King Hezekiah (2 Kings 18–20), we can receive hope during our own troubles—from the most political to the most personal. When we think of Jesus living up to the names in Isaiah 9:6, we can turn to our Lord for wise counsel, mighty faith, intimate prayers to our Father, and a peace that passes understanding. Once again, the prophet Isaiah—perhaps the most eloquent figure in the Scriptures—gives us a larger gospel by which we can seek to embody the kingdom of heaven on Earth. Similar expansions of the gospel take place in relation to Isaiah 11, Isaiah 35, and Isaiah 61. When we see Jesus fulfilling these prophetic visions in the way the Gospels portray, we can experience what Jesus said to many prophets and other righteous people who "longed to see" (Matthew 13:17), and we can share that royal experience with our suffering world.

Then, with grace upon grace (John 1:16), we can bring to our suffering world not only an anointed king but also a suffering servant. We can witness to and seek to embody a Messiah-Christ who is also "a man of suffering and acquainted with infirmity." (Isaiah 53:3). And we can also note that when we see Jesus fulfilling Isaiah 53, we see him fulfilling what scholars call "the fourth servant song" in the book of Isaiah.

In Isaiah 42, the same Lord who has promised a descendant of David who will rule all nations (Isaiah 11:1–10), now promises a "servant, whom I uphold, my chosen in whom my soul delights." (Isaiah 42:1 NRSV). This servant will receive the Spirit of the Lord (a form of anointing), and he will "bring forth justice to the nations." (Isaiah 42:1b NRSV). Astonishingly, this hoped for servant "will not cry or lift up his voice or make it heard in the street." (Isaiah 42:2 NRSV). Instead, "a bruised reed he will not break, and a dimly burning wick he will not quench." (Isaiah 42:3 NRSV), and yet he will establish "justice in the earth." (Isaiah 42:4 NKJV). This amazing servant is one of the "new things I [the Lord] now declare." (Isaiah 42:9 NRSV).

In Isaiah 49, a second servant song appears, and now the Lord emphasizes that the servant will do God's work not only among the already chosen people but also among peoples living without the light of God's Word. Speaking to people in need of their own rescue, the Lord enlarges his gospel by stating, in regard to his servant, that:

> "It is too light a thing that you should be my servant to raise up the tribes of Jacob and to restore the survivors of Israel; I will give you as a light to the nations, that my salvation may reach to the end of the earth." (Isaiah 49:6 NRSV).

According to the third servant song in Isaiah 50:4–11, this salvation will be earth-wide and come through a servant who experiences blows to his back and the tearing out of his beard. (Isaiah 50:6). Instead of hiding his face from insults and spitting, the servant sets "his face like flint" and trusts the Lord to vindicate his person and his work. (Isaiah 50:7). While these servant songs may not be as familiar to many Christians as the passages from Isaiah 7, 9, and 11, they did play a crucial role in Jesus' understanding of his person and mission. As Jesus preached the kingdom of God and ministered in a way that brought heavenly power to Earth, he did so with a mind informed by the servant songs in Isaiah. Luke observes as Jesus "set his face to go to Jerusalem"

(Luke 9:51), he did so knowing that he would face great suffering and rejection as well as execution. Still, Jesus also knew that after his crucifixion, "on the third day he would be raised." (Luke 9:22). That trusting knowledge of resurrection came to Jesus via the servant in Isaiah, of whom the Lord said, "See my servant shall prosper; he shall be exalted and lifted up, and shall be very high." (Isaiah 52:13 NRSV). That brings us to the fourth, final, and in many ways ultimate servant song, which appears in Isaiah 52:13–53:12.

In the fourth servant song, the Lord speaks in a way that, in part, describes the people of God exiled into Babylon and in a way that, even more, describes the mind and work of Christ. The Lord's servant sends a message to nations, and he calls all people to believe that God saves through a descendant from the root of Jesse. (Compare Isaiah 11:1, Isaiah 11:10 and the "root" in Isaiah 53:2). When it comes to a nation humiliated by exile or to a person despised on a cross, people can wonder who could believe good news from God. And yet as we listen to God's Word, we learn that "he was wounded for our transgressions and crushed for our iniquities." (Isaiah 53:5 NRSV). In the unexpected and even unimaginable plan of God, "the will of the Lord" includes his beloved servant crushed "with pain", and yet "out of his anguish he shall see light" and we shall be made righteous. (Isaiah 53:10–11). As people made right with God by the sacrifice of God's servant, we can seek to participate in God's plan to set all things right.

When we read the New Testament Gospels in dialogue with the servant songs, we begin to share the mind of Christ. (See Philippians 2:5–11). Having read Isaiah, we understand that Jesus was able not only to predict his passion (Mark 8:31, 9:31, 10:33), but he was also able to live it out. By God's Word and Spirit, Jesus knew he could glorify his Father by dying like a seed and being lifted up on a cross. (John 12:20–36). Jesus knew and incarnated the suffering love of God by being lifted up—first on a cross, then from the tomb, and finally to the right hand of his Father. (See John 12:32 and 20:17). From the right hand of his Father and our Father, Jesus makes "intercession for transgressors" (Isaiah 53:12), and as we realize those transgressors include us, we not only receive grace but also share it. We can care for God's world by coming into lives and situations "not to be served but to serve" (Mark 10:45), and like our Anointed King Suffering Servant Jesus, we can bring good news and God's presence not only in terms of the forgiveness of sins but also in the form of whatever forms of justice and mercy bring healing. With all God's people, we can confess, "by his bruises we are healed" (Isaiah 53:5 NRSV), and we can relate the whole gospel to the entire world by living as wounded healers. Isaiah's prophetic vision as fulfilled by Jesus Christ makes for a larger gospel and a larger salvation. It offers a striking picture of Israel's ideal promised King, who has come already in grace and will come again in glory.

## A Note of Joy

At the outset of this chapter, I reflected on Dr. Josef Hromádka teaching the Scriptures in terms not only of themes, but even more of motifs. At the end, we can reflect on how the eloquent prophet Isaiah speaks to both our afflictions and our hopes with such subtlety that we hear not only themes and motifs, but also earthly tones and heavenly music. Thanks to Isaiah's preview and portrait of our Savior, even in our darkest and scariest times, we can overhear "good news of great joy." (Luke 2:10). We can feel close to the lowly shepherds who heard "a multitude of the heavenly host, praising God and saying, 'Glory to God in the highest heaven, and on earth peace among those whom he favors.' " (Luke 2:14 NRSV).

# Chapter 6

## Eschatology for a Wide Salvation

"He is the image of the invisible God, the firstborn of all creation; for in him all things in heaven and on earth were created, things visible and invisible, whether thrones or dominions or rulers or powers—all things have been created through him and for him. He himself is before all things, and in him all things hold together. He is the head of the body, the church; he is the beginning, the firstborn from the dead, so that he might come to have first place in everything. For in him all the fullness of God was pleased to dwell, and through him God was pleased to reconcile to himself all things, whether on earth or in heaven, by making peace through the blood of his cross."   (Colossians 1:15–20 NRSV).

> "After this I looked, and there was a great multitude that no one could count, from every nation, from all tribes and peoples and languages, standing before the throne and before the Lamb, robed in white, with palm branches in their hands.  They cried out in a loud voice, saying, 'Salvation belongs to our God who is seated on the throne, and to the Lamb!'" (Revelation 7:9–10 NRSV).

## The International and the Interpersonal

As I have sought a larger gospel, I have found that we must draw upon the one or more particular forms of Christian ministry in which we serve or have served. In my case, as is true for others as well, my own choices have played a subordinate role to where God's call has led me. I have two ministerial colleagues who have devoted their entire ministries to preaching and pastoral work, each in just one congregation, and that is a fruitful field for labor. Other colleagues have served not only in different congregations but also in distinct types of ministry, and that pattern describes my experience. I have served in denominational settings, in preaching and pastoral positions, in social ministries that operate mostly independently (primarily after retirement), and in teaching the Bible at denominational colleges. In addition to those various settings, I served for over twenty years as a military reserve chaplain and also participated in two short-term team mission trips to Siberia. All these experiences contribute to how I understand the gospel, and they prompt me to explore biblical material having to do with Jesus as the one who fulfills the vision in Daniel 7 of "the Son of Man." Before turning to that material, I will pass on more information that can help us connect our interpersonal experiences to the international character of the gospel.

During one of my missional trips abroad, I was in Russia. While there, a lady employed in the hotel where I was staying expressed a wish to have "a serious talk" with me about her grandson. When we sat down together, she immediately brought the conversation to a serious level regarding this loved one in her life. After listening, I felt free to offer this thought to her: "I can pass on to another only what I find true for myself." She certainly saw the point and agreed. As we exchanged ideas, she responded well, and we had a serious talk about Christ in her life - leading the way to one of the first changes of heart in our team ministry! Later, we both were ready to talk further about her grandson.

Such concern for others can open the door for a deeper examination of one's own spiritual resources. Perhaps it should go without saying, but I would encourage any reader interested in the forms of the gospel to appraise the validity of my conclusions as a prelude to suggestions on sharing the faith. I believe it also may be said, however, that where we find a door tightly closed to the Christian concepts of human sin, we may experiment a little to encourage rather than put a stop to conversations. When an opportunity for sharing the faith comes along, and I find clear resistance in a friend to discuss matters of human sin, I might tiptoe into another area of deep human need to which other Scriptures point, such as relationships ranging from the most personal to the most global.

However "correct" a particular theology may be by scriptural standards and theological analysis, it has very little value for human lives unless we engage others in it in a way that elicits personal passions. If we personally assimilate from theological analysis benefits only for ourselves and fail to incorporate them into active sharing of the gospel, do we not limit our usefulness both for the life of the church and the mission to those outside of Christian circles? On the other hand, when we find the larger gospel actually addressing not only human sin but other deeply profound problems of the human predicament, we thereby increase our options in how we can reach individuals for Christ and the gospel—both on the side of human need and on the side of the redemptive actions of Christ that meet those needs. Thus, even as we recognize our responsibilities beyond evangelism, the larger gospel opens to us new options in the way we do the work of evangelism, whether informally, one on one, or in an appointed role of Christian leadership.

Those with responsibility for leadership in preaching, evangelism, pastoral care, worship, and overseas missions may find it helpful to experiment a bit in how they might apply the message of this book most effectively in their respective fields of responsibility. Growing recognition of the additional gospel forms could benefit individuals, as well as inject new power, confidence, and a larger common purpose into the church of the twenty-first century. In bringing the apostolic gospel and the gospel of the rule and kingdom of God closer together, I see an enhanced unity of the New Testament message, whether conveyed academically, apologetically, or evangelistically. In whatever form, the point is to recognize the humanity and the personhood of whomever God brings into your life. To offer biblical material in support of such efforts, we can turn to the book of Daniel—and in particular the prophet's vision of "the Son of Man."

## Daniel and the Humane Kingdom of God

Daniel is probably best known as someone thrown into a lion's den and centuries later sung about by countless children in Sunday school. (You can find various versions on YouTube.) Without denigrating either the biblical stories or the children's songs associated with Daniel, we can focus on the vision Daniel receives in chapter 7 of the book that goes by his name. This vision, which includes a heavenly "Son of Man", will help us envision and seek a humane expression of the kingdom of God on Earth.

As Daniel 7 begins, the exiled character Daniel is portrayed as living and serving during "the first year of King Belshazzar of Babylon." (Daniel 7:1). Having managed to achieve social standing while surviving persecution (see Daniel 1), Daniel still identifies primarily with his Jewish people—a people who suffered humiliating defeat and cruel exile at the hands of the Babylonian empire. As Daniel lies in bed in that setting, he receives "a dream and visions" (Daniel 7:1) that reveal the hidden but true sovereignty of the God of Israel, even during times that could seem hopeless for the chosen people.

In Daniel's dream, "four great beasts came out of the sea", and these beasts represent "four kings [who] shall arise out of the earth." (Daniel 7:3, Daniel 7:17 NRSV). Scholars have various views of the exact identities of the four beasts—a debate related to different views of the authorship of Daniel—but all readers can agree that these kings act with a cruelty that is worse than beastly, for they can dehumanize the enemies they defeat. And that critique applies especially to the fourth beast- wielding a horn that represents a persecuting empire. In the vision given to Daniel, the horn "made war with the holy ones and was prevailing over them." (Daniel 7:21 NRSV).

The key point for us to see in Daniel 7 is that when God takes decisive action against imperial evil and on behalf of his saints, God acts through "one like a son of man". Through this figure, who is simultaneously heavenly, human, and humane, God overcomes imperial evil and instead gives dominion, glory, and kingship to the son of man, who shares his power with "all peoples, nations, and languages." (Daniel 7:13, 14, 27 NKJV). In this way, the mysterious son of man brings a kingdom similar to that promised to the descendants of David in passages such as Isaiah 9 and 11—a kingdom in which people are free from fear and free to love. And although Daniel does not fully comprehend the vision he receives—in fact, he states, "my thoughts greatly terrified me," (Daniel 7:28 NRSV)—still, Jesus fulfills the vision by combining the title "Son of Man" with Isaiah's vision of a Messiah who is also a Suffering Servant. (See the material on Isaiah in the previous chapter.)

Sometimes when people read about Jesus referring to himself as the "Son of Man", they interpret the title in terms of the theological teaching that Jesus is perfectly human as well as perfectly divine. And even though that theological point is correct, it is not what Jesus intends in his use of the title. Instead, when Jesus refers to himself as the "Son of Man", he reveals that he not only has solidarity with human beings but he also brings heavenly power to Earth in order to save us. In a word, he fulfills the vision of Daniel 7. To give just two examples of many possible ones regarding this title, we can turn to these passages in the Gospel of Mark.

In Mark 10, Jesus' disciples are competing for power and glory in all-too-human terms. In response, Jesus teaches the truly human and humane way of greatness by stating, "...whoever wishes to be first among you must be slave of all. For the Son of Man came not to be served but to serve, and to give his life as a ransom for many." (Mark 10:44–45 NRSV).

In Mark 10, we see Jesus combining the title "Son of Man" with the message of the Suffering Servant, and in Mark 14, we see Jesus combining both these teachings with the title Messiah. As priests, elders, and other religious authorities interrogate Jesus, finally "the high priest asked him, 'Are you the Messiah [the Christ], the Son of the Blessed One'"? (Mark 14:61 NRSV). Note that Jesus responds in a way that leads both to the cross and to the fulfillment of God's many promises. He says, "I am", and echoing both Psalm 110 and Daniel 7, he adds, "and 'you will see the Son of Man seated at the right hand of Power' and 'coming with the clouds of heaven'." (Mark 14:62 NRSV).

For making this bold claim, Jesus suffers condemnation to death on a cross, but he also receives vindication by his resurrection from the dead. The point for us to see in our search for a larger gospel is that as the Son of Man, Jesus acts in a way that brings God's heavenly and humane kingdom to Earth. As opposed to competitive kingdoms (or societies) in which the desire for power can lead to cruelty, Jesus brings a communal kingdom in which the will to serve leads to love. In the tradition of Daniel, John, the author of Revelation, receives a vision in which he sees Jesus as "one like the Son of Man." (Revelation 1:13 NRSV). As the Son of Man, Jesus shares sovereign rule on Earth with his Father in heaven, and he works in such a way that: "The kingdom of this world has become the kingdom of our Lord and of his Messiah, and he will reign forever and ever." (Revelation 11:15 NRSV).

Such is the wide and winsome good news that takes place because Jesus comes to us as Messiah, Suffering Servant, and Son of Man.

## Apocalypse Now

At this point, we should pause and note that both Daniel 7 and the book of Revelation communicate with us in a genre that is called "apocalyptic literature." In apocalyptic literature that is inspired by God, our Lord reveals or, so to speak, "unveils" his saving plan in a way that gives hope for the future and also direction for the present. In terms of giving direction for the present, Jesus' fulfillment of the apocalyptic figure, "Son of Man", leads us to respect and live in solidarity with every human being. This is because every person not only reflects the image of God (Genesis 1:26–28) but also participates in the human family, which now includes Jesus—who is both the Son of God and Son of Man.

When I think of following Jesus as the Son of Man in terms of what the Scriptures teach, one passage central to my thoughts is the judgment story Jesus tells, which we often call "the parable of the sheep and goats." (See Matthew 25:31–46). Initially, this parable can frighten us because it portrays "the Son of Man" (Jesus) as coming to us in the form of the hungry and thirsty, strangers, the naked, the sick, and the imprisoned. Then Jesus proclaims that if we ever neglect to help such people, he could view us as goats and sentence us to eternal punishment. (See Matthew 25:41–46). But if we recognize that Jesus uses judgment language to startle and awaken us so that we will follow him, we can hear the parable as a message from the Savior who goes on to die for our sins. Therefore, we can receive the parable as an inspiration to live out the gospel in every relationship, especially with those in need. In other words, all of us sometimes help the needy, at which times we act like sheep, and all of us sometimes neglect the needy, at which times we act like goats. Our Good Shepherd Jesus startles us in the direction of living as sheep. In sum, Jesus gives us his vivid parable, and at the same time comes to us as our crucified and risen Lord and Savior, and in this way, he inspires us to encounter him among "the least of these who are members of my family." (Matthew 25:40 NRSV). So at this point, I will pass on some related experiences and exhortations regarding encountering Jesus among a variety of fellow humans.

During most of my retirement years, my wife and I participated actively in an independent evangelical congregation, and we took part in its internal hosting and teaching ministries. We chose the degree of variety only in a limited sense since ultimately it is the Lord who arranges our relationships. Where God calls us is the determining factor, and we heard God calling us into this form of service. The point for all of us is that whatever ministries and relationships into which God calls us, we must use them to gain the special perspectives God gives us—perspectives that teach us to understand and apply the good news in the widest way possible for us.

All such experiences certainly enable me to look with different eyes upon the diverse strands of relationships God has been opening to me as the years of my life progress. I did not plan for my life to unfold as it did, and on the surface, some might view it as a hodgepodge of professional assignments. But somehow God wove the diverse strands of my personal history together into a gospel-expressive story, and in the course of preparing this book my labor brought me back to my first love among the Christian disciplines: the Bible and its theology. In a virtuous circle, the Bible led me into various ministries and then the ministries led me back to the Bible, where I found a larger gospel that brings good news to persons from every background.

In the further pursuit of the concerns of this book and its challenging problems, I have suggested that a greater and more irenic communication between those of different traditions and backgrounds could very well prove helpful to those who want to grow in their knowledge of our Lord. I have had in mind here not only traditions that are theological in nature but also those that represent different approaches to life in a broader sense, for instance. Among them such traditions as mentioned in Richard Foster's book, *Streams of Living Water: Essential Practices from the Six Great Traditions of Christian Faith.* As Foster artfully enumerates and describes these traditions, they go as follows: the contemplative tradition, the holiness tradition, the charismatic tradition, the social justice tradition, the evangelical tradition, and the incarnational tradition. Of course, within these traditions, there have been numerous sectarian movements in theology that have wandered far from the material and formal principles just mentioned—often by overemphasizing particular teachings at the expense of others. However, those upholding Scripture and Christ's relating principles can recognize misleading distortions when they arise and contend against them, both decisively and in a gentle Christian spirit. The great reward of such an irenic and ecumenical attitude will be that Christians can practice all six streams, even when they feel called in particular ways to focus on one or two of them. In his book, Foster powerfully portrays Jesus as embodying all six streams.

The example of Christ in combination with Foster's winsome book can widen our experiences and practices of Christian spirituality. From personal experience, I can testify that drawing upon these various streams while combining them with Christian activities and service keeps us from being armchair Christian observers. Instead, we find our Lord drawing us out of isolation and into partnership with people from all kinds of backgrounds who share the name of Christ. I recommend reading Foster in dialogue with your Bible reading as a way to provide space for the Holy Spirit to do his work in your life and in the lives of those around you. To give a personal example, as an American who, thanks to Jesus the King-Servant Son of Man, I have had good relations with Christians from the United Kingdom and other nations, and I can testify to the Son of Man working in this way to gather all nations to himself (Matthew 25:32).

## Combinations, Personhood, and Stewardship

Having explored both the Old Testament and the New Testament, and having seen how Jesus fulfilled all God's promises in the Scriptures by combining the titles of Messiah (or Christ or King), Suffering Servant, and Son of Man, we can now explore how we can combine our biblical studies and our personal experiences into practical embodiments of the gospel. The highly specific lesson that will emerge is the practice of stewardship, or giving. As we explore further teachings from the apostolic gospel of Paul, we will find him teaching us how to live out the Kingdom gospel in a way that includes the imitation of Christ. And that combination will, in turn, enable us to live out our versions of both the death and resurrection of Christ.

In 1 Corinthians 12 (and also in Romans 12 and Ephesians 4), Paul invites his readers to use for God and fellow believers the full range of gifts and talents that God has entrusted to them. Paul especially encourages the higher or more needed gifts in the life of the Church because this is the best way "members" can help "the body of Christ", which is a primary Pauline metaphor regarding the Church. Christians have made application of Paul's principles and teachings here to a wide range of stewardship practices, such as the stewardship of the "three T's"—talent, time and treasure. Combining these three T's helps us understand Paul's message regarding the many different ways in which God may call each one of us, using the particular functions of the human hands, feet, ears, etc., each without duplication, but instead as ways of supplementing the others. In Romans, Paul teaches members of Christ's body "not to think of yourself more highly than you ought to think, but to think with sober judgment, each according to the measure of faith that God has assigned." (Romans 12:3). In this way, Paul teaches a genuine humility by which we can also recognize our own gifts in order to share them with others.

Such sharing of gifts uncovers latent gospel components such as reconciliation and transformation. In these latent but central gospel teachings, we discern how our relationship to God as a Person inspires and informs our relations to human persons in a way that includes our stewardship. That is to say, the particular niche in which we may realize ourselves as belonging to God shapes the way in which we cultivate right relationships between ourselves and our fellow human beings. Such cultivation certainly includes every conscious and communal response to his love toward us. As Paul puts it, "God, who is rich in mercy, out of the great love with which he loved us even when we were dead through our trespasses, made *us alive together* with Christ..." (Ephesians 2:4–5 NRSV, italics added). Clearly, we may apply such solidarity teachings to all human relationships as well. Again, we have the remarkable saying from Matthew 25:40 (KJV) to inspire and instruct us: "...Inasmuch as ye have done it unto one of the least of these my brethren, ye have done it unto me."

With respect to living out these teachings in the specific practice of giving, a central guiding passage comes in 2 Corinthians 8–9. In these chapters, the Apostle Paul teaches generosity to a troubled church by pointing to the example of Christ, who lived out the gospel of the kingdom. As Paul encourages his brothers and sisters in Corinth to give financial support to needy members in the body of Christ in Jerusalem, he states:

> "I do not say this as a command, but I am testing the genuineness of your love against the earnestness of others. For you know the generous act of our Lord Jesus Christ, that though he was rich, yet for your sakes he became poor, so that by his poverty you might become rich." (2 Corinthians 8:8–9 NRSV).

The words above translated "generous act" are a fitting rendition of the Greek word "charis", which is typically translated as "grace." The point for us to see here is that Paul, with his apostolic gospel of grace, leads his readers to Jesus, who incarnates the Kingdom gospel of justice. As we receive Paul's teaching that "God loves a cheerful giver" (2 Corinthians 9:7), we will find ourselves enabled to live out Jesus' teaching to "not worry" but instead "strive first for the kingdom of God and his righteousness." (Matthew 6:25, 33 NRSV).

**The Personal Outcome of the Gospel**

We can conclude this chapter by connecting the sometimes abstract teachings of theology and economics to the core biblical teaching of personhood. From the Old Testament days into the New Testament era and beyond, the people of God have, at their best, understood the gospel as a personal message that transforms every personal relationship, from the most intimate to the most global. An ancient Israelite psalmist speaks for all people who see salvation in a person when he writes,

> "The LORD is my light and my salvation;
>    whom shall I fear?
> The Lord is the strength of my life;
>    of whom shall I be afraid"?
> (Psalm 27:1 NRSV).

Therefore, it should not surprise us that we also see our salvation in the very person of God. As with the psalm, so with the New Testament: The gospel message is that as we connect with the Person of God, we need not fear the threat of enemies; instead, we can ask, "If God is for us, who is against us"? (Romans 8:31 NRSV). And if we wonder whether we can bear the cost of discipleship, we can trust the reward of discipleship to come from the God "who did not withhold his own Son, but give him up for all of us." (Romans 8:32 NRSV). When we consider a Three-Person God who made such sacrifices on our behalf, we can rejoice when Paul teaches, "...you are not your own. For you were bought with a price; therefore glorify God in your body." (1 Corinthians 6:19, 20 NRSV).

Perhaps the best way to tie the teachings of this chapter together is to recall the future Apostle Paul on the road to Damascus. Saul, a person we could label as a religious terrorist, spent his days "breathing threats of murder against the disciples of the Lord." Then, when Jesus encountered this violent zealot, our Lord did not ask, "Why do you persecute my followers"? Instead, Jesus asked, "Saul, Saul, why do you persecute me"? (Acts 9:1-4 NRSV). Paul met the person Jesus—the second Person in the Trinity—when he met fellow persons such as Stephen and Ananias. (See Acts 8:1 and 9:10). Therefore, when the converted Paul wrote to his fellow believers in Corinth about their quarrels, he did not ask, "Has the Church been divided"? Instead, he asked, "Has Christ been divided"? (1 Corinthians 1:13 NRSV). And when he explained membership with the metaphor of a body, he did not say, "So it is with the Church." Instead, he said, "...so it is with Christ." (1 Corinthians 12:12 NRSV).

How humbling and yet ultimately liberating it is to consider that the way we treat fellow Christians is the way we treat Christ. And how sobering and yet ultimately empowering it is to consider that the way we treat the least is the way we treat Jesus. When we combine the apostolic gospel of Paul with the Kingdom gospel of Jesus, we find ourselves receiving and sharing personhood as gracious gifts from the Tri-Person God. We find ourselves united in work and prayer with "...God our Savior, who desires everyone to be saved and to come to the knowledge of the truth."  (1 Timothy 2:3–4 NRSV).

# Chapter 7

## The Holy Spirit and All Truth

"I still have many things to say to you, but you cannot bear them now. When the Spirit of truth comes, he will guide you into all the truth; for he will not speak on his own, but will speak whatever he hears, and he will declare to you the things that are to come. He will glorify me, because he will take what is mine and declare it to you. All that the Father has is mine. For this reason I said that he will take what is mine and declare it to you." (John 16:12–15 NRSV).

### Both/And Regarding Trust and Obey

Sometimes two people can listen to the same hymn and have widely divergent responses. Other times, a person can encounter a Bible passage early in life and ignore it, and then remember it later in life and feel transformed. We can call this a "both/and" view of the gospel and the Christian life. A word such as "trust" can feel like both an impossible demand and a doorway to peace. It can depend on the person who hears the word. A word such as "obey" can seem irrelevant to someone with certain priorities, and vitally important to the same person later in life. We can have such phenomena in mind as we claim a larger gospel by letting the "Spirit of truth" lead us into "all the truth" (John 16:13), but before we explore such biblical teachings regarding the Holy Spirit, I will put some flesh on the topic by passing on some personal experiences and reflections.

Some readers may receive the lyrics to "Trust and Obey" as overly didactic, but for me that song will always bring back memories of listening with my mother to her little radio in her room at a nursing home. I fondly recall the last moments we ever would have to share in its entirety a song that would always have special meaning to me. As we were saying our goodbyes, my mother seemed in good health, and we paused happily to sing together the strong message of the song's lyrics, most of which we knew by heart. Little did we realize that this would be the farewell song of our lives together—I would never see her alive again. In 1973, which was in the days before the variety of instant communication we have today, we were at the Grand Canyon when I finally received word that my mother had gone home to her Lord. When we reached my son's home in California, we held a small family service in her memory. So in one sense, I am speaking about past events, and in another sense, I am reflecting on present and permanent realities. At that time, that song—and especially its two great words, "trust" and "obey"— became forever engraved in my memory. I came to see the hymn as a special communication from the Lord and

Savior my mother and I both loved and sought to serve. What had once been a song of happiness grew into a song of eternal joy.

By the gift of the Holy Spirit, similar experiences of grace can take place in countless ways. And from our side, acknowledging that God always has a larger purpose than we can imagine opens us up to depending upon and working with God in the direction of "all the truth", from the most personal to the most cosmic. So in this chapter, we will look at some biblical teachings regarding the ever-expansive ways of God, and we will look at various ways we can respond to and participate in God's progressive revelation. While recognizing that this process can take a long time to develop, we can live already with the glowing hope expressed by the psalmist: "And he shall bring forth thy righteousness as the light, and thy judgment as the noonday." (Psalm 37:6 KJV).

## The Holy Spirit in John and Beyond

According to the Gospel of John, when the Word—the Second Person in the Trinity—became flesh in Jesus Christ, he came with light and life and also experienced darkness in the form of rejection and opposition. (John 1:1–11). That rejection and opposition would eventually lead to condemnation and crucifixion, so Jesus—a unique person but also as fully human as his followers—welcomed his Father's gift of the Holy Spirit. In relation to Jesus, John the Baptist testified, "I saw the Spirit descending from heaven like a dove, and it remained on him." (John 1:32 NRSV). And with grace upon grace, Jesus not only received the Holy Spirit but he shares it with us. As John the Baptist again testified (this time by quoting our Father in heaven): "He on whom you see the Spirit descend and remain is the one who baptizes with the Holy Spirit." (John 1:33 NRSV). So in order to claim a larger gospel, we must explore the gift of the Holy Spirit.

One window into the illumination and vitality of the Spirit comes in Jesus' conversation with a person named Nicodemus (John 3:1–21). In the original Greek of his Gospel, the writer John identifies Nicodemus as "a man, being a person of the Pharisees." (John 3:1). That designation enables us to see Nicodemus both as a person like us and as a person who comes from a particular subculture. This makes him both distinct from us and also like us since we all come from particular subcultures.

Nicodemus initiated the conversation with Jesus and attempted to flatter our Lord by saying to Jesus, "Rabbi, we know that you are a teacher who has come from God; for no one can do these signs that you do apart from the presence of God." (John 3:2). Jesus then responded with sharp words that functioned as a scalpel to open Nicodemus to new life. Jesus answered, "Very truly, I tell you, no one can see the kingdom of God without being born from above." (John 3:3 NRSV). And when Nicodemus expressed perplexity, Jesus cut even further by declaring, "Very truly, I tell you, no one can enter the kingdom of God without being born of water and Spirit." (John 3:5 NRSV). With those words to Nicodemus, Jesus raised questions for all of us:

1. Have I been born from above (or born again)?
2. Have I been born of water and Spirit (or baptized by the Holy Spirit)?

By rephrasing Jesus' questions into questions that have occupied and even divided Christians for many centuries, we can open our minds to encounter the Gospel of John's teachings in personal and communal ways. For example, we can identify with Nicodemus and realize that even "a teacher of Israel" or a lifelong Christian can always grow in understanding. Similarly, someone baptized as an infant into a truly Christian home can always grow in faith. These claims ring true for those seeking to claim a larger gospel because they help us view being born again as a lifelong process of dying and rising with Christ. (See Romans 6). They also help us understand baptism with the Holy Spirit as a lifetime of drinking from the deep and wide fountain of the Holy Spirit. When we receive the light and life of

Jesus by his Holy Spirit, we realize we never understand exhaustively even the truths we learned in Sunday school. Instead, every day we can continue "...to believe that Jesus is the Messiah, the Son of God, and that through believing [we] may have life in his name." (John 20:31 NRSV).

To get a feel for how the Holy Spirit gives us continual life and light, we can listen in on Jesus' "Farewell Discourse" in John 14–16. That passage, which portrays Jesus speaking to his disciples in an upper room before suffering betrayal and crucifixion, reveals the highly encouraging truth that when Jesus gives his Holy Spirit to us, the Spirit comes as what the Gospel, in its original Greek, calls "the Paraklete." In the ancient world, a paraklete was someone who came alongside you when you called out for help. A paraklete would then give you whatever form of help you most needed—encouragement, counseling, conviction, or some combination of all these and more. So it is inspiring to consider that Jesus sends the Paraklete as "the Spirit of truth." (John 14:16–17). Jesus sends the Paraklete as the Spirit who teaches and reminds us of everything Jesus gives us to know (John 14:26), to testify to Jesus acting on our behalf (John 15:26), and to continue his work in the world and to guide us into all truth (John 16:5–15). And with respect to us, by the gift of the Spirit, participating in Jesus' cosmic work of truth, we can look at another scene in the Gospel of John.

In John 20, after appearing first to Mary Magdalene, the risen Jesus returned to his failed disciples and said, "Peace be with you." (John 20:19). After speaking words that announced forgiveness and restoration, Jesus showed wounds that revealed compassion and love. The Gospel of John then provides a humble and quiet version of the Great Commission (see Matthew 28) and Pentecost (see Acts 2). As his disciples rejoiced, Jesus repeated his greeting of peace and then stated, "As the Father has sent me, so I send you." With the word "send", Jesus commissioned his disciples to continue his work on Earth, and with his next action he empowered them for a mission that would be otherwise impossible. John tells us, "When [Jesus] had said this, he breathed on them and said to them, 'Receive the Holy Spirit. If you forgive the sins of any, they are forgiven them; if you retain the sins of any, they are retained'." (John 20:21–23 NRSV).

By foreshadowing the wind and fire of the Acts 2 Pentecost, Jesus' breath of life invites us to participate in the John 20 Pentecost. Like the disciples, we can receive and share the forgiveness Jesus gives to us. Like the disciples, we can receive and share the Holy Spirit. Like the disciples, we can discern how forgiveness and justice go together. By knowing both, we can understand that forgiveness brings liberating power and opens the way for possible reconciliation. Knowing that some sins need additional attention for the sake of protecting the vulnerable and doing justice for all, we can carry out our version of the Great Commission as we claim and share a larger gospel. To accomplish that, we can both pray for the Holy Spirit and also "...test the spirits to see whether they are from God." (1 John 4:1 NRSV).

## One Body, Many Members

By the time we read 1 John, the community of the Apostle and Evangelist John has experienced what Jesus foretold in his Farewell Discourse. Fellow members of the people of God have persecuted them with the same spirit by which they persecuted Jesus. The Holy Spirit, as Paraklete, has helped John's community withstand such opposition, and the Paraklete has enabled them also to remember and stay near to their Lord. (See John 15:18–16:3). On top of experiencing expulsion from their synagogues, the Johannine community has also suffered division within itself. Some seemingly "spiritual" members of their community have felt led to deny "that Jesus is the Christ." (1 John 2:22). John's community is able to discern the nature of this error because they "have been anointed by the Holy One" (1 John 2:20), and in that way, the Holy Spirit has already been at work to lead the Church into all truth: The incarnate Jesus, who suffered the seeming defeat on the cross, has actually risen and begun decisively his work to "draw all people to [him]self." (John 12:32). Only now the arms that were nailed to the cross have become arms in the body of Christ we call the Church. And the body of Christ can continue the work of Christ because the same Spirit that empowered Jesus now empowers us.

When we consider the work of the Spirit in such terms, we can think further in terms of both the Kingdom gospel of Jesus and the Resurrection gospel of Paul. When it comes to the Kingdom gospel and Jesus, we can think first of how, in all four Gospels, John the Baptist promised that the one following him would baptize "with the Holy Spirit." (Mark 1:8; cf. Matthew 3:11, Luke 3:16, and John 1:33). Like "a fountain flowing deep and wide", the Spirit descends on about one hundred twenty people on Pentecost, and soon grows the church by thousands (Acts 2:41). From that dramatic but still small beginning, the Spirit has empowered the Church to live out Jesus' promise that we would be his "witnesses in Jerusalem, and in all Judea and Samaria, and to the ends of the earth." (Acts 1:8 NRSV). The gospel truth today is that when Christians meet even in groups of two or three, the Spirit unites us with billions of other Christians across the globe.

When it comes to the resurrection gospel and Paul, additional truths related to the Holy Spirit emerge.

In ways that the Jerusalem disciples could not yet imagine, the Holy Spirit had led Gentile believers into a direct relationship with the God of Israel. It turned out that Gentiles in the city of Thessalonica were as beloved and chosen as any other member in the Abrahamic family of faith (1 Thessalonians 1:4). And to live fully as a member of the family of faith, Gentiles did not need to obey all the laws of Moses—as beautiful as they are. Instead, they simply needed to believe the gospel Paul preached to them (Galatians 3:1–5). And that belief is not simply an intellectual adherence to a set of teachings; rather, it is a vibrant union with the living Christ, by which the Spirit creates a "faith working through love." (Galatians 5:6). As the Spirit engenders faith in believers in Christ, the Spirit also distributes gifts by which they can live together as the body of Christ (1 Corinthians 12). As members of the body of Christ, believers follow the most "excellent way" of love as Paul describes in his justly famous chapter, 1 Corinthians 13. As we seek to embody such love and to claim and live out a larger gospel, we will follow Paul's additional teaching: "Pursue love and strive for the spiritual gifts, and especially that you may prophesy." (1 Corinthians 14:1 NRSV). This final Spirit-led truth we can now ponder seeking to understand what the gospel means by prophecy, tongues, and all the gifts of the Spirit. This will inspire us into a never-ending pursuit of the fullness in Christ, because when we open ourselves to such a mystery, we receive power to "...be steadfast, immovable, always excelling in the work of the Lord, because [we] know that in the Lord [our] labor is not in vain." (1 Corinthians 15:58 NRSV). How fascinating that the Spirit leads us into this and all truth.

## We Believe and Grow in Belief

For a final section in this chapter, we can consider how the Spirit leads us into an always developing faith and how such growth relates to the earlier theme of a gospel that is both overt and latent. We can note with astonishment that the Holy Spirit, who leads the whole Church into all truth (John 16:12–16), also speaks to each of us personally. Because the Spirit bears witness to our spirits, each of us can call on the Creator of the universe as Abba, Father (Romans 8:16).

When it comes to the Spirit leading us into all truth by means of an always-growing faith, we can think again of Jesus' Farewell Discourse in John. In loving and moving final words before the cross, Jesus speaks to his disciples as people who believe in him, and as believers who need to grow in faith. For example, when Jesus washes the feet of his disciples, he tells Peter, "You do not know now what I am doing, but later you will understand." In a similar way, Jesus tells all the disciples, "Where I am going, you cannot come." (John

13:7, 33 NRSV).  The disciples cannot follow Jesus on his way to the cross because they cannot yet comprehend that Jesus will return to his Father by being lifted up in that way.  Toward the end of the Farewell Discourse, the disciples experience a breakthrough in part when they understand Jesus' words more clearly and confess, "Now we know that you know all things, and do not need to have anyone question you; by this we believe that you came from God."  In response to that strong expression of faith, Jesus asks, "Do you now believe"?  And then Jesus answers his own question by stating, "The hour is coming, indeed it has come, when you will be scattered, each one to his own home, and you will leave me alone."  (John 16:30-32 NRSV).

Again the disciples believe in the sense that they know Jesus comes from God, but they cannot believe— they cannot comprehend—that he will return to his Father by being lifted up on a cross.  For all disciples and believers, it takes our entire lives to comprehend the connection between Jesus being lifted up on the cross, being lifted up from the grave, and finally being lifted up to the right hand of our Father in heaven, who, as the risen Jesus states to Mary Magdalene is "my Father and your Father … my God and your God."   (John 20:17).  The inescapable truth of the gospel is that because the gospel is so large, we live as people of little faith.  (See Matthew 8 and 14).  As Paul says, we "know only in part" (1 Corinthians 13:12), and that partial knowledge limits our faith. But by his Spirit, Jesus enables us to grow stronger in faith. One way we can participate in that growth is to trust Jesus when he prays to his and our Father. "I made your name known to them, and I will make it known, so that the love with which you have loved me may be in them, and I in them." (John 17:26 NRSV). Jesus offers that prayer on behalf of everyone who believes in him because of the message of the apostles (John 17:20). That prayer means that every time we read the Gospel of John, and every time we grow in the gospel truth at all, we increase our belief, and at the same time we grow in faith. Therefore "...through believing [we] may have life in [Jesus'] name." (John 20:31 NRSV).

When it comes to having and sharing life in Jesus' name, we can grow as we return to the theme of the overt and latent character of the gospel. We can certainly give thanks for all the overt ways in which we speak of the gospel. When we gather for Gospel readings in public worship, when we read the Gospels with loved ones or in our personal studies, and when we share the gospel by speaking to people about Jesus in explicit terms, these are all overt expressions of the gospel. At the same time, when we experience any labor or encounter any person who makes us alive, when we feel awe in relation to any work of art of a scene in creation, and when we trace whatever elicits passion in us back to God as the Giver of all gifts, these and countless other graces are latent experiences of the gospel. And by holding these themes—overt and latent—together, we enjoy a larger gospel and follow Jesus as the Holy Spirit leads us into all truth. We participate as the Spirit of Jesus leads us from a receptive level of faith (which never ends) to a commitment level of faith (which always grows). We become the good soil that Jesus describes in his parable of the sower: "...these are the ones who, when they first hear the word, hold it fast with an honest and good heart, and bear fruit with patient endurance." (Luke 8:15 NRSV). While always learning to believe from children who trust our Father wholeheartedly, we also live out Paul's words: "When I was a child, I spoke like a child, I thought like a child, I reasoned like a child; when I became an adult, I put an end to childish ways." (1 Corinthians 13:11 NRSV). Mature faith means abiding love.

# Part Three
## Making the Claim

## Chapter 8

## The Church and Its Creeds

"I ask not only on behalf of these, but also on behalf of those who will believe in me through their word, *that they may all be one*. As you, Father, are in me and I am in you, may they also be in us, so that the world may believe that you have sent me. The glory that you have given me I have given them, *so that they may be one, as we are one*, I in them and you in me, that *they may become completely one, so that the world may know that you have sent me and have loved them even as you have loved me*. Father, I desire that those also, whom you have given me, may be with me where I am, to see my glory, which you have given me because you loved me before the foundation of the world.

"Righteous Father, the world does not know you, but I know you; and these know that you have sent me. I made your name known to them, and I will make it known, so that the love with which you have loved me may be in them, and I in them." (Jesus' prayer for his followers in John 17:20–26 NRSV; italics added).

## The One Pearl and the Many

I was born and raised in the Protestant tradition. As I grew in years, I came to learn of divisions within Protestantism, such as the Fundamentalist–Liberal controversy that raged especially in the early twentieth century, but had expressions both before and after that time. As I grew in my faith, I came to understand these divisions as differences that we need not deny and yet can overcome through the one gospel as we claim it in its larger form. For example, although I am a Protestant, I feel deeply indebted to mysticism, which has outstanding expressions within the Roman Catholic tradition. Also, Roman Catholic worship included contemplative prayer, apostolic proclamation of the Scriptures, healthy practices for Christian nurture, and an abiding concern for the poor. This last emphasis has taken concrete expression in remarkable systems of institutional networks and services. Such realities have parallels within Eastern Orthodoxy and other traditions such as Coptic or Syrian Christianity. Such truths lead me to seek embodiment in Paul's instructions to all Christians, as summarized in his exhortation:

"I therefore, the prisoner of the Lord, beg you to lead a life worthy of the calling to which you have been called, with all humility and gentleness, with patience, bearing with one another in love, making every effort of maintaining the unity of the Spirit in the bond of peace. There is one body and one Spirit, just as you were called to the one hope of your calling, one Lord, one faith, one baptism, one God and Father of all, who is above all and through all and in all." (Ephesians 4:1–6 NRSV).

Having heard Paul's apostolic exhortation to unity, we can expand on it by thinking imaginatively in one of Jesus' kingdom parables. For me, this parable took on new life as I came to appreciate friendships and learn from people even when they had views in conflict with my own. As dialogues and even debates led me to valuable insights and inspiring examples, I found myself hearing a version of an old claim in relation to living the gospel today. Rather than saying, "Yes, Virginia, there is a Santa Claus", I was led to state, "Yes, Virginia, there is a pearl of surpassing value." That pearl is the kingdom of heaven on Earth, which helps us to put every other pearl in its proper place. That pearl is Jesus himself.

In Matthew 13, Jesus tells a series of parables that reveal glimpses of the kingdom of heaven coming to Earth. In one kingdom parable, he tells of a "merchant in search of fine pearls." (Matthew 13:45). According to our Lord, "on finding one pearl of great value, he went and sold all he had and bought it."

(Matthew 13:46). By placing ourselves within that brief word picture, can we find one gospel pearl of surpassing value? The answer is yes. By reflecting deeply and sincerely on Jesus' metaphor with respect to questions and issues in our own lives, we can find the kingdom of heaven on Earth and the King who blesses us with belonging.

When we ask, "Could there be one pearl so valuable that it outshines all other gems?" we can begin by exploring the answers that various Christian traditions have offered. Within the bounds of even Western Christianity, we can find many conflicting answers. In some traditions, the key truth emerges in the sacrament of the Lord's Supper. Others have claimed exclusive truth in their understanding of baptism. In some cases, groups have rallied and divided with respect to social justice issues; in other cases, the critical issue has to do with personal holiness. Some have argued for an uncompromising teaching regarding biblical infallibility while others have insisted on a strict, as opposed to "worldly", lifestyle, and the list of differences could go on.

In my search for a larger gospel, I have seen the significance of these and other issues, but I do not see any one of them in isolation as amounting to the pearl of great price on which the unity of the Church depends. Instead, we can treasure these lesser pearls by viewing them in light of the greatest pearl, our Lord himself. For example, in the following two statements from Jesus, we see him insisting not on one particular teaching but, instead, on one Person:

> "He called the crowd with his disciples, and said to them, 'If any want to become my followers, let them deny themselves and take up their cross and *follow me*. For those who want to save their life will lose it, and those who lose their life *for my sake*, and for the sake of the gospel, will save it'."
> (Mark 8:34–35 NRSV); italics added).

> "Jesus said, 'Truly I tell you, there is no one who has left house or brothers or sisters or mother or father or children or fields, *for my sake* and for the sake of the good news, who will not receive a hundredfold now in this age—houses, brothers and sisters, mothers and children, and fields, with persecutions— and in the age to come eternal life'."
> (Mark 10:29–30 NRSV; italics added).

In relation to this Person-Pearl of infinite value, we need not discard every other pearl. Instead, we can work together to put them in proper relation to one another. In this way, we can live out Jesus' prayer for us in John 17, that we would be one. That has been my experience, and I have encountered many versions of the same story, as I have claimed a larger gospel by studying the history of the Church.

## One Tree, Multiple Branches

As the Apostle Paul sought to live out Jesus' prayer that the Church would be one, he dealt with painful realities in the body of Christ. For example, in relation to the church he founded in Corinth, he received a report from "Chloe's people that there are quarrels among you." In seeking to prevent such quarrels from growing into permanent divisions, Paul asked, "Has Christ been divided"? (1 Corinthians 1:11-13 NRSV). For Paul and for all believers in Jesus, the ultimate and eternal answer to the question is no. But sadly, in its "not yet" historical existence, the body of Christ has experienced divisions so painful that in light of 1 Corinthians 12, with its metaphor of one body with many members, we can speak of dismemberments that we can seek to overcome.

One early controversy that would lead to dismemberment was the earliest Church's debate regarding how believers in Christ stood in relation to the covenant God made with Israel through Moses at Mount Sinai. Some Jewish Christians insisted that as Gentiles came into the renewed Israel created by Christ, they needed to follow Jewish teachings. Subsequently, some individuals from Judea told the newly born members of Christ, "Unless you are circumcised according to the custom of Moses, you cannot be saved." (Acts 15:1–2 NRSV). That claim generated controversies that were overcome in part by the Council of Jerusalem, as described in the rest of Acts 15. As Christians today seek unity in accord with the Spirit of that Council, we can find much insight from the Apostle Paul in Romans 14–15. In those chapters, again in relation to how members of the body of Christ stand in relation to the teachings of Moses, Paul deals with what we can call "disputable matters."

According to the Apostle, when fellow believers differ, some of them can hold stronger positions and other weaker positions, and yet we need not despise or pass judgment on one another because "God has welcomed" all those who have faith in Christ. (See Romans 14:1–4). Paul asks each and all of us, "Why do you pass judgment on your brother or sister? Or you, why do you despise your brother or sister"? To help us answer such questions with humility, Paul states, "For we will all stand before the judgment seat of God." (Romans 14:10 NRSV). As we consider that "each of us will be accountable to God" (Romans 14:12), we can find motivation to "pursue what makes for peace." (Romans 14:19). We can live out Paul's inspiring exhortation: "Welcome one another, therefore, just as Christ has welcomed you, for the glory of God." (Romans 15:7 NRSV).

In my efforts to welcome and seek unity, I have found rich resources in the Church's teachings regarding the triune God. One way the Holy Spirit fulfilled Jesus' promise to lead us into all truth (John 16:12–15) was to inspire the Church to formulate the Nicene Creed. Amid much dialogue and also fierce debates in the 300s and 400s after Christ, the Spirit led Church Fathers to formulate a creed, based on biblical verses, that tells Christians that we believe in one God, the Father Almighty, one Lord Jesus Christ, the only Son of God, and one Holy Spirit, "the Lord, the giver of life."    (I would encourage readers to research the Nicene Creed at this time).   When believers today and in every age consider that we know God as Three Persons and yet one God, we can seek to live out Jesus' prayer for oneness in John 17 by obeying his command regarding love in 1 John 4.  In that passage, the Spirit of Christ inspired John to write:

> "Beloved, let us love one another, because love is from God; everyone who loves is born of God and knows God. Whoever does not love does not know God, for God is love.  God's love was revealed among us in this way: God sent his only Son into the world so that we might live through him. In this is love, not that we loved God but that he loved us and sent his Son to be the atoning sacrifice for our sins. Beloved, since God loved us so much, we also ought to love one another.  No one has ever seen God; if we love one another, God lives in us, and his love is perfected in us." (1 John 4:7–12 NRSV)

Seeking to love in imitation of the Triune God, who is love, shapes my view of Church history and calls me to ecumenism. For example, when I think of the split between the Latin Western Church and the Greek Orthodox Church in 1054, even the word over which these two branches of the one tree split—the word "filioque", which means "and the Son"—becomes a source of unity for me. The Latin West insisted on adding "filioque" to the Nicene Creed in order to proclaim that "the Holy Spirit proceeds from the Father and from the Son" and that claim regarding Christ and the Spirit opens me to unity in spite of disagreement. When we approach dialogue with genuine openness to what the Spirit may yet have to say to the Church, we are open to developments that can transform hurtful divisions into creative differences. That is one way for me to claim a larger gospel.

The same ecumenical truths and Spirit apply to another division in the Church that took place about 500 years later—what we call the Protestant Reformation, beginning with Martin Luther's 95 Theses in 1517. As Luther discerned something drastically wrong in the Church practice of selling indulgences, he searched the Scriptures for saving truths and was led to conceptual and theological insights that inspired the doctrine of justification by faith alone. Although the term *sola fide* (by faith alone) does not appear explicitly in Paul's letter to the Romans, Luther did discern teachings in Romans that led him to develop a radicalized and still biblical version of Paul's teachings regarding justification and faith. As Augustine had done centuries earlier, Luther found in Paul's ancient words a living testimony to God's unconditional acceptance of him, even though he was a sinner. And as we inherit Luther's teachings regarding *simul iustus et peccator* (simultaneously right with God and a sinner), we can find in that teaching the grace and humility we need to unite with other Christians, even when we formulate our teachings with different emphases. Roman Catholics and Greek Orthodox Christians have taken major steps toward unity in the past fifty years or so and so have Roman Catholics, Lutherans, Reformed Christians, and others. The Spirit of John 16:12–15 can use even divisions to lead us into all truth. As I study Church history, the larger gospel I find there leads me to believe that underlying all areas of theological differences, there should be a genuine openness to what the Spirit may have to say to the development of the Church's beliefs and practices, of its inner life and integrity, and of the power and influence of its outward witness. After all, Jesus prayed that we would be one "...so that the world may believe that you [the Father] have sent me." (John 17:21 NRSV).

### Not (Exclusively) Technical Theology

In conclusion to this chapter on the Church with its creeds as a source not for division but for unity, I can mention a personal anecdote that related to the highly personal practice of marriage. As in the first century, so in our 21st centuries some Jewish people are led to put their faith in Jesus Christ, and when they do so, they can differ on how much to maintain regarding ancient

162

Jewish traditions. For example, I attended a wedding where one of the principals was Jewish and wished to follow a number of older Jewish traditions in the ceremony. The underlying belief at work in that context was the view that differences between Jewish Christianity and Gentile Christianity have to do with secondary customs that we can view in the perspective of Jesus as the Jewish Messiah for people from all backgrounds. Some Jews that convert to Christ are led to affiliate with Gentile Christian congregations; other Jews that convert are led to affiliate with Jewish Christian congregations. When we practice theology in a Christ-centered way, we can know that they all live by the same gospel for the one Lord. Such deeply personal results from theological thinking alert us to the true nature of theology.

For many people, the very word "theology" is construed as a technical term that elicits interest from only a scholarly few. I hope my writings indicate that theology can actually serve as a life-giving resource for anyone wanting to meet God in the Scriptures and in an always-growing gospel. In my case, the discipline of theology and several specific theologians have helped me make room for the Holy Spirit to breathe new life. Without being chained to traditions, we can call on teachers in various traditions to help us hear the Bible as a whole. In the next chapter, I will share how theologians have expanded my understanding and faith and helped me begin to claim a larger gospel.

# Chapter 9

## Theology and Theologians

"Hear, O Israel: The Lᴏʀᴅ is our God, the Lᴏʀᴅ alone. You shall love the Lᴏʀᴅ your God with all your heart, and with all your soul, and with all your might." (Deuteronomy 6:4–5 NRSV).

"You shall love the Lord your God with all your heart, and with all your soul, *and with all your mind.*" (Jesus, regarding the greatest commandment, Matthew 22:37 NRSV, italics added).

"...yet for us there is one God, the Father, from whom are all things and for whom we exist, *and one Lord, Jesus Christ*, through whom are all things and through whom we exist." (1 Corinthians 8:6 NRSV, italics added).

## Hearts and Minds

Often and rightly, we speak of different kinds of loves. In his book, *The Four Loves*, for example, C.S. Lewis writes about charitable love, erotic love, friendship love, and familiarity love. These loves are indeed distinct, but they almost always work together in some way. The same truth applies to the different love commandments Jesus speaks of in his summary of the commandments of God. (See Matthew 22:24–40). Standing in line with all God's prophets, Jesus teaches that love for God and love for our neighbors are distinct but inseparable. And by implication, he teaches a similar truth about love with our hearts and love with our minds. (See the quotations above, which introduce this chapter; notice how Jesus develops the love commandment as presented in Deuteronomy 6). As we seek to claim a larger gospel, we find ourselves obeying both what Jesus calls "the greatest and first commandment" of loving the Lord our God and also the second to love our neighbors as ourselves, which, according to Jesus, is "like it." (Matthew 22:38-39). When we truly love God with everything we have, we inevitably love our neighbors as ourselves. And when we love our neighbors with our hearts, we cannot help but love God with our minds. As Paul says, love "binds everything together in perfect harmony." (Colossians 3:14 NRSV). That has certainly been my experience.

During my years of pastoral, social and teaching ministries—combined with overseas team missions—numerous issues have come to mind, and they all relate to my work in Christ's name with people. Although my work with the gospel has not been exclusively at the conceptual level, it has involved conceptual considerations. Sometimes new thoughts have led to new actions, and sometimes new actions have led to new thoughts. That virtuous circle has also characterized my preaching and teaching—both in groups and with individuals, at home and abroad. This theological dynamic has encouraged me to claim a larger gospel, and I trust it will offer similar encouragement to you as well. Theology is both an academic discipline and a universal way of thinking about how God and life go together. And in this case also, we can both distinguish and separate. Even if you choose not to major in theology, you can do some major theological thinking as you follow your Lord. This will lead to surprising experiences of renewal at the levels of both understanding and practice.

### Excellent Example: Eldon Ladd

For me, a theologian named George Eldon Ladd has provided both academic and everyday inspiration in the practice of theology. After receiving ordination as a Baptist minister, Ladd worked as a pastor in mostly Evangelical circles before earning a doctorate in New Testament studies at Harvard University—a school open to but very different from Evangelical perspectives. Bridging different perspectives continued for Ladd when, in 1950, having completed his Ph.D. dissertation, he took a position at Fuller Seminary in Pasadena, California. There, Ladd helped Fuller expand the Fundamentalist movement in the United States into a broader Evangelical movement that allowed for scholarly excellence. At their best, Evangelical scholars help their students and communities love the Lord with both their hearts and minds. And in the case of Ladd, this combination took place mostly in the realm of eschatology, the study of the last things.

Early in my life as a Christian and in my education as a theologian, I encountered elaborate systems of eschatological speculation that distorted gospel teachings. Too often opinions of theologians regarding the precise sequence of events leading to the age to come were emphasized above the glorious promises of what God has in store for us. Also too often, the opinions of such theologians regarding eschatological details were turned into litmus tests for others regarding their orthodoxy. Such antagonisms led to unhealthy divisions and the sad formation of new denominations. In that context, Ladd interpreted New Testament teachings with a level of perception that few could match. Ladd's book, *Jesus and the Kingdom*, had the subtitle *The Eschatology of Biblical Realism*. His scholarly work regarding these and numerous themes in the Scriptures had a real effect on me and many others. It helped us anticipate the gift we will experience in full at the end of the age, when Christ will gather all his people in a united experience of his righteousness, love, purpose, and power. Ladd helps us understand in part and practice the consummation of the gospel, when God will be all in all.

In my reading of Ladd's most notable works, I learned to connect the biblical term usually translated "kingdom of God" with an equally valid translation of "reign" or "rule" of God. Although I will continue to use the common translation "kingdom", I encourage my readers to join me in seeking to understand how Jesus looked at the kingdom. That will open our hearts and minds to what the gospel meant to Jesus during his Galilean ministry and what it means for us in our lives with God today.

Jesus' view of such central terms as "gospel" and "kingdom" has been the subject of debates that go back centuries. In Ladd's time, Albert Schweitzer felt sure that Jesus' gospel of the kingdom would not find realization in the here and now, but only in the mysterious age to come. On the other hand, C.H. Dodd mostly dismissed futuristic speculations about an age to come and focused on what is often called "realized eschatology", which takes place here and now. Both Schweitzer and Ladd present their strong thoughts in compelling ways. Schweitzer helps us imagine Jesus coming to us in a mystical way and saying, "Follow thou me." Dodd inspires us to hear the gospel with all the public authority of a medieval town crier. In response to these strong yet opposing views, Ladd seeks the best from both. On the basis of passages such as Matthew 12:28 and Luke 17:21, Ladd developed what we can call an "inaugurated eschatology", in which God's promises and Jesus' kingdom revelations do indeed begin here and now, while also including beyond imagined realities that will reach perfection in the age to come. To summarize the teachings of Ladd and others in his camp, students of theology often speak of the "already and not yet" character of the gospel. The kingdom of God (a world of heaven on Earth) has begun already, and it is not yet fulfilled perfectly. Such an "already but not yet" perspective contributed to the dynamism of Jesus' life on Earth, and that dynamism can continue in our lives.

For example, as followers of Jesus, we pray every day, "Your kingdom come; your will be done on earth as it is in heaven." (Matthew 6:10 NRSV). When we rise to live out that prayer, we, in communion with Christ, can participate in all kinds of works that spread "already": health, new life, and help for the poor. The truth that realities such as sickness, death, and poverty are "not yet" eliminated need not lead us to lose heart and give up. Instead, we can already translate our longing for the kingdom into ways that we express Jesus' rule right now. We can carry out some version of what Jesus did in Galilee. Since Jesus died, rose, and poured out his Spirit, what he began during his days on Earth continues through the work of the Church and through the work of everyone who does what is right. What Jesus began in his earthly ministry, he continues through his apostles and through all who share their belief in Jesus and his gospel. (See Acts 1:1–4).

To give just one more example of how Ladd's teachings—both in terms of background and in terms of specific passages—can help us claim a larger gospel, we can look at how the Gospel writer Matthew summarizes Jesus' ministry in an early portrait of his work in Galilee. The eloquent but in some ways aging translation known as the King James Version presents Matthew 4:23 as follows: "And Jesus went about all Galilee, teaching in their synagogues, and *preaching* the gospel of the kingdom, and healing all manner of sicknesses and all manner of disease among the people." (Italics added). Current leading English language translations such as the NIV and NRSV restate this verse by using a more comprehensive term for "preaching", as in, "*proclaiming* the good news of the kingdom." (Italics added). The point is that in these more recent translations, "preaching" is subsumed under the broader term "proclaiming."

This seemingly small change opens up a world of possibilities. One of them is that "preaching" usually refers to the spoken word. In contrast, "proclaiming" includes preaching but also refers to other modes of communication, such as acting out, as in a drama, or speaking in different genres, such as a parable. Most central to Jesus' proclamation of the kingdom was his practice of putting the kingdom into flesh-and-blood action as he healed the sick, fed the hungry, stilled storms, and so on. With that broad understanding of proclamation in mind, we can better understand Jesus' response to the inquiry from John the Baptist as to whether he truly was the Messiah. Jesus was able to say, "Go and tell John what you *hear and see.*" (Matthew 11:4 NRSV, italics added). Heartfelt theology such as we encounter in Ladd's works helps us to embody a gospel that people can "hear and see." By reading about theologians such as Ladd, we can put ourselves into Gospel stories set in Galilee, and we can claim and live out Gospel stories in whatever place God has led us to live.

## One Who Prays and Does

One saying that reflects my holistic view of theology is a saying that has been attributed to various Church Fathers: "A theologian is one who prays, and one who prays is a theologian." I know the Church Fathers and all good theologians would agree when I expand the saying to include "one who does"—that is, one who lives out what one prays. Earlier in this book, I gave indications of this truth, and I can review them briefly here:

In his "Foreword", David Moberg kindly testifies to how our theological conversations contributed to his work as a social scientist. Having founded a group called "Theological Confab", I can testify to how our discussions about Christ can make us more effective in our work for Christ. In my "Preface", I build on that insight by describing how reading theology in the works of Dallas Willard helped me avoid narrowing the gospel into a mere "sin management" and, instead, expanded into a mission that encompasses all of life. Possibly no recent writer has equaled Dallas Willard regarding the consistency with which he presses the point that the gospel call is incomplete unless it leads to an ensuing life with Christ that encompasses everything in life. In a work such as *The Great Omission,* Willard illumines wonderfully how the gospel includes transformation into a new life. Willard helped me live out childhood songs that taught transformation more than I realized at the time. I remember singing to the beautiful tune of Braham's "Lullaby" simple and profound words that say, "Keep our lives free from sin and our hearts pure within." Such liberation and purification last a lifetime, and Willard helped me understand that.

As we saw in chapter 4, we were able to learn much from Gustav Aulén regarding the difference atonement theology makes in our everyday struggles against threatening tyrants, and these are only a few explicit examples of how theologians have helped me throughout this book and in my entire life. For a more recent discussion of atonement teachings, you can read Paul Fiddes' book, *Past Event and Present Salvation: The Christian Idea of Atonement.* Such authors and books are beginning to add up, so as I mention a few additional names and themes, I offer them not as requirements but simply with the hope that you can find practical help by engaging in theological studies.

A friend of Dallas Willard named Richard Foster wrote an inspiring book called *Streams of Living Water: Essential Practices from the Six Great Traditions of Christian Faith.* As the subtitle indicates, in this work, Foster brings out the fruit of good theology in at least two ways: He describes "essential practices", and he shows how "great traditions" in our faith flow from the same source and toward the same goal—Jesus Christ, the Alpha and the Omega. In a highly helpful way, Foster explores several theological traditions, not in order to find the one "correct" view, but in order to extract truth irenically from them all. From Foster's book, we can all find a starting point to draw on historical and theological traditions less familiar to us than our own. I recommend this book highly, along with other works by Foster. Readers may also want to consult an organization Foster and Willard helped to found called "Renovare." The theologians associated with Renovare can help you find renewal in your life with God.

For any readers who may want to expand and update kingdom eschatology as taught by Ladd, a theologian named Brian Vickers provides an article called "The Kingdom of God in Paul's Gospel." Reading Vickers' work will help you grasp both the Jesus gospel and apostolic gospel, and it will help you live them out in ways both overt and latent. If you are willing to go back a generation or two, Gerhard Kittel can illustrate the major biblical theme of redemption, ransom, and related teaching, and he does so with various images that can open our imaginations even further. Kittel wrote near the time that I was reading Karl Barth and meeting personally with luminaries such as Barth, Paul Tillich, and Reinhold Niebuhr, and their influence continues to this day. In our own time, a preacher named John Piper has written and spoken in a way that can help you find joy in a life dedicated to the glory of God. Similarly, a preacher named Tim Keller can speak to common contemporary questions about God while testifying to the City of God taking form in our midst. Another teacher, named Scot McKnight, can help us discern Jesus as the true King, in contrast to false claims from false royals, and while I could go on at much greater length, I trust these names can lead you to other names, so I will conclude by mentioning here only one more theologian: Bernhard Anderson. In his studies of the Exodus and the Old Testament as a whole, Anderson helps us experience the gospel in larger and liberating ways. He and other theologians, both named and unnamed, have led me places beyond what I expected when I began to study them. They have also helped me understand why the divisions in the Church need not be permanent but, instead, can be overcome by deeper and wider theological dialogues. I hope my testimony here can encourage you to explore some form of your own "theological confab."   In my case, further explorations of theology led me to sing "Songs of the Kingdom" with joy.   For that musical expression of a "theological confab" located in Milwaukee and dating from 2014, I received inspiration and assistance from my son, Dwight Jaggard.

# Chapter 10

## Hopes for the Future

"Then I saw a new heaven and a new earth; for the first heaven and the first earth had passed away, and the sea was no more. And I saw the holy city, the New Jerusalem, coming down out of heaven from God, prepared as a bride adorned for her husband. And I heard a loud voice from the throne saying,

> 'See the home of God is among mortals,
> He will dwell with them;
> they will be his peoples,
> and God himself will be with them;
> he will wipe every tear from their eyes.
> Death will be no more;
> mourning and crying and pain will be no more,
> for the first things have passed away.'

And the one who was seated on the throne said, 'See, I am making all things new'. Also he said, 'Write this, for these words are trustworthy and true'." (Revelation 21:1–5 NRSV).

### Claiming the Larger Confab Choir

Having mentioned assistance and inspiration from my son Dwight, I can speak of others who can participate in the practice of "theological confab"—

including you. For example, Sherri L. Teale also provided assistance with respect to singing in a way that reflects Jesus' theology of God's kingdom, and mentioning her name points us also to a larger choir or "multitude that no one could count." (Revelation 7:9). Claiming a larger gospel has given me a preview of the vision that, according to John the Seer in Revelation, awaits us all. When worshiping "...in the Spirit on the Lord's day" (Revelation 1:10), John received a series of visions, including several moving depictions of the new creation God has in mind for us. In one vision, John sees people "...from every nation, from all tribes and peoples and languages, standing before the throne and before the Lamb, robed in white, with palm branches in their hands." (Revelation 7:9 NRSV). John describes this congregation as crying out "in a loud voice" in praise of God, and also falling on their faces in worship and singing:

> "Amen! Blessing and glory and wisdom
> and thanksgiving and honor
> and power and might
> be to our God forever and ever! Amen."
> (Revelation 7:12 NRSV).

My assured hope is that we can begin to join in such crying out and singing as we worship on Sundays, as we pray together every day, and as we gather in some form to hold a theological confab. In fact, that would be one way to describe this book: a theological confab by means of which we draw closer to one another as we draw closer to our Lord. In my view, as we allow God to have his way with us, not only through the Scriptures but also through our prayers and confabulations, we will begin to experience what God has in mind for the rest of this century and for the eternal world to come. I trust that since you are reading this book, you share some version of that hope.

## Further Investigations via Dialogue and Experience

As we approach the conclusion of this book together, I find myself fascinated by the possibility of further investigations of the issues we have covered explicitly or discussed in implicit ways. So once again I call on the distinction between theology as an academic discipline and theology as a way of life, and I invite you to consider further investigations either in an academic or a comprehensive manner. What are some topics for your possible exploration? And what are some ways to investigate? Here are some brief observations and suggestions.

The topics mentioned in the previous pages (e.g., the kingdom content of the gospel, the latent form of the gospel, the theme of redemption in the Scriptures, etc.) have such richness to them that further study would prove highly worthwhile. A related observation regarding these and any issue that emerges is that we need not limit our explorations to the Scriptures or to the Christian tradition. Instead, in dialogue with Paul's message to the Athenians from the Areopagus, we can understand that all kinds of people worship what Greeks in Paul's day called "an unknown god." (Acts 17:23). On the basis of that inscription, which Paul saw carved into an altar for worship, the Apostle appealed to his listeners by quoting from a pagan poet who searched after God by writing, "In him we live and move and have our being." (Acts 17:28 NRSV). As we grow in faith by claiming a larger gospel, we can see such a statement not as a threat to gospel truths but as an invitation to share those truths by means of dialogue. The traditional term for such a starting point is "general revelation", and in our day of global interaction, general and special revelation can hardly avoid coming into dialogue with one another. How fascinating it is to consider that everyone whom we encounter almost certainly has some awareness of God.

Christians on the mission field occasionally describe encounters with people that truly are searching for truth and for God. Sometimes these people have never even heard the name Jesus; other times they have heard the name but only in some negligible or distorted manner. The point for us to see is that whether we identify as missionaries or not, we can often witness immediate responses to the Christian message once such people receive the message in a meaningful way. As I think about such encounters, which can overflow with love and joy, I find myself encouraging you to explore such connections either by manner of study, manner of dialogue, or both. To carry out such explorations, we can call on the Roman Catholic teachings regarding natural theology (often more positive than Protestant teachings), and we can develop a more dynamic concept of God's revelation. By entering into an ever more dynamic dialogue with God through the Scriptures, history, and experience, we can offer what N.T. Wright calls "signposts" to God's future. We cannot offer people an advance photograph of God's future, but we can point to it with the kind of humility and hope that can lead people of every background to open their minds to God. We can call this a form of the "latent gospel", as it offers a winsome alternative to the anxiety and confusion all too common in our culture.

As I describe such a broadminded view of revelation, and way of relating to others, I do so aware of biblical verses and doctrinal teachings that could seem to demand a stricter approach. But as theologian Reinhold Niebuhr reminds us, it turns out that engaging with such perspectives in a dialogical way will help us overcome our own tendencies toward pride and other forms of evil, which can distort our best intentions. What we can call a "dialectical motif" in relation to teachings and relationships flows out of the Bible and helps us claim a larger gospel. Anyone who studies the Scriptures seriously will soon discover apparent contradictions in the Bible itself (e.g., different passages lay different emphasis on the importance of faith and works with respect to salvation from God). What can Christians do with such seeming contradictions? The answer is to see that each can be correct when we factor in the full sense and context of the passages. To say that all truth is on one side of a debate and to dismiss the other side simplistically is to miss the fullness of God's truth. A dialectical way of proceeding says that one passage can be true in one sense while another is true in another sense. And when we emphasize the passages in Scripture that call us to God-centered views of revelation and salvation, we will actually find ourselves more, rather than less, attentive to human responsibility. For instance, when we see ourselves saved in relation to God by grace alone, we find ourselves free and even compelled by love to act in saving ways toward our fellow human beings. God does not need our good works, although he delights in them. Our neighbors do need our good works, sometimes at the level of life or death. Keeping these two truths in dialogue with one another makes for a more dynamic faith and life.

A few other "both/and" issues are worth mentioning because they could stimulate readers to practice a dynamic understanding of God's revelation. For example, in one sense it is true that Jesus' parables typically have one central point. In another sense, it is also true that Jesus' parables have unlimited interpretations. So, for example, imagine reading the parable of the prodigal son when you are young and have gone dangerously astray. Then imagine reading it when you have acted in a way that you view as responsible and feel frustrated (like the elder brother in Luke 15) when an erring child receives a profligate welcome home. And finally, imagine living as a parent with different children lost in different ways; imagine seeking to discern how to love them and how to help them get along. To engage in such contemplation of

181

Jesus' parables is to rest in the central truth of grace, while also opening your mind to limitless expressions of love. Such a "both/and" view can help us engage in daily and lifelong dialogue and partnership with God.

Another "both/and" factor to mention by way of review and encouragement is that both the apostolic (Pauline) and kingdom (Jesus) forms of the gospel witness to the one Lord Jesus Christ, who is the same yesterday, today, and tomorrow, while also relating to us with a beauty that is ever ancient, ever new. (See Augustine for further exploration of such beauty in God). By noting both the multiplicity and the oneness of our Savior, we walk in the footsteps of the early Church, which rejected the idea of reducing the four Gospels into one summary document. Instead, early catholic teachers preserved the four portraits of Matthew, Mark, Luke, and John, and that act of preservation has encouraged ever expanding creativity. The Light of the World can always open our eyes and minds to more light and more glory. When we take this "both/and" approach to the Scriptures, the creeds, and the various Christian traditions, we will always find a larger gospel to claim. Things the Bible says implicitly, we can say explicitly, and the virtuous cycle never ends. Explicit developments of biblical teachings will help us discover meanings and metaphors in the Bible that we had missed earlier. It is yet another way to live out the passage we explored earlier—John 16:12–15—in which Jesus promises that the Holy Spirit will lead us into all truth. That leading continues, and that is good news in itself.

Finally, to speak briefly and open mindedly about a divisive contemporary issue, we can mention that we can explore the Scriptures in dialogue with disciplines such as psychology, sociology, history, literature, and philosophy. When we do that, we can take an attitude similar to that which Pope Francis takes in dealing with people regarding human sexuality. Francis, while seeking to make Church teachings on love and mercy central to the Church's message, also asks, "Who am I to judge?" Such humility adds to the power of gospel teaching, and it opens ways for us to disagree while remaining united in love. In that regard, we can all learn from John the Baptist, who desired people to listen, first of all, not to him but to Jesus himself. John the Baptist compared himself to the joyful friend of a bridegroom and said of Jesus Christ, "He must increase, but I must decrease", (John 3:30 NRSV). Such humility emerges as we claim a larger gospel, which always gives more glory to Christ and the Triune God, who is love.

To conclude this section on a practical and positive note, we can observe that the humility of a "both/and" approach to Christ can give us harmony and peace as we pray and worship. For example, while Christians debate—sometimes so fiercely that these debates have been called "worship wars"—the place of "praise songs" in Christian worship, we can see the appeal in such songs while not abandoning traditional hymns and instead developing music that expresses the fullness of Trinitarian teachings. Our God is both Three and One. How can our worship testify to such a mysterious and revealing God unless we take a "both/and" view toward how we sing, how we pray, and how we gather together? Consider both the many mighty acts of God and also the central teachings of the gospel. Should not both and all these truths be embodied in the songs and liturgies—be they formal or informal—of weekly worship?

Finally, as we practice that perspective in every aspect of worship, we can give it particular priority as we celebrate the Lord's Supper. Traditionalist theologies have often drawn hard and fast lines in relation to teachings such as transubstantiation, consubstantiation, real presence, etc. The treatment of any solution to these huge debates goes far beyond the scope of this book. At the same time, central themes in this book point to ways not so much of solving the issues but of living with them in a unified way. We can ask, what purpose did Christ have in mind when he said, "Do this in remembrance of me"? Did he want us focused on theoretical teachings that never exhaust the mystery of the sacrament? Or did he want us focused on the way his body and blood lead us to the cross? And what happens when we survey the wondrous cross on which our Savior died? To quote the magnificent hymn by Isaac Watts, we "pour contempt on all our pride." Instead of seeing error in one another, we unite in the beauty of a love and sorrow mixed that brings us all together into shared love and joy. Paul echoes such themes when he writes, "For as often as you eat this bread and drink the cup, you proclaim the Lord's death until he comes." (1 Corinthians 11:26 NRSV). When we focus on such a truth from Paul and the Truth itself in the Person of Christ, we feed our souls and grow in faith. We participate together in the present love and coming glory of our Lord.


## Same Cloth and New Cloth

My search for a larger gospel has taught me much about both unity and readiness. For example, both the Scriptures and experience have taught me that faith and hope are of the same cloth. So while I feel certainty regarding my trust in the Lord to bring salvation to its ultimate perfection, I have no knowledge of the Lord's timing in the completion of his work to make all things new. Therefore, I have both faith and hope in part, and I know that the love of Christ will empower both these virtues to endure. They are of the same cloth; they are distinct but related perspectives on reality, and they prompt me to seek new cloth in terms of readiness for change and development. Keeping such truths together helps me to follow Jesus. On the one hand, our Lord tells us that he came not to abolish but to fulfill the law and the prophets (Matthew 5:17–20), and that brings out the unity of the Old and New Testaments; on the other hand, Jesus warns us against sewing a new and unshrunk piece of cloth onto an old cloak, "...for the patch pulls away from the cloak, and a worse tear is made." (Matthew 9:16 NRSV). So Jesus wants us to live both faithful to the one true God of our ancestors in the family of faith, and he wants us ready for when the Lord does new things. In regard to matters of both faith and hope, we can seek to live like the wise bridesmaids in Matthew 25. We can keep our lamps trimmed and burning, and we can be ready for the bridegroom when he comes. (See Matthew 25:1–13). Unity and readiness for change go together as we seek a larger gospel with love.

For me, the same cloth of unity and new cloth of readiness came together in a recent experience I had with a new church friend who had an uncertain faith. As I came to know this man, I did so as someone who has known the Lord and his gospel since my childhood. My faith in the Lord and his gospel has remained steady for decades while also growing throughout that time. That combination helped when my friend entered a time of crisis.

After two years of promising recovery sparked by active participation in the fellowship and responsibilities of church life, things came apart for my friend on a single night. Having been called upon by his family to settle a dispute, he made the serious mistake of bringing a gun to the volatile scene. As someone on parole, merely carrying a gun was a problem in itself. Then, out of fear of the police, who also arrived at the scene, my friend engaged in an exchange of shots and found himself in prison that very night for violating his parole.

My wife, Jean Dale, and I visited him in the county jail while he was awaiting trial. I think we all recognized that his recent actions would result in him having to serve time in jail again. He listened when I spoke with him of Christ's love and the gospel. I said to him something like this: "If you receive a sentence again, I don't want you to wake up each morning thinking that the big thing in your life is that you are in prison. I want Jesus Christ to be the big thing in your mind and heart." My friend listened and seemed to accept this message as a word from the Lord. In fact, despite his trying circumstances, he expressed loving concern for a woman at church who had suddenly and unexpectedly lost her husband. That expansion of a human heart is an example of the larger gospel in action.

The term "big thing" was not the usual way of referring to the gospel, and it is certainly not direct biblical language, but my friend knew what I meant, and my choice of words caught his attention. Before we left, he made his first direct commitment to Christ. Several things had come together and interacted: the preaching of the gospel he had been listening to over the past two years, the witness and lives of Christians around him, his own development of the skills necessary for taking on responsibilities in one of the regular Sunday morning ministries, and other factors as well. But finally, it was a restating of the Scriptures in everyday terms that apparently opened the door to Christ for him. That incident provides for me a striking example of what such restatements of Scripture can accomplish with respect to communicating the good news. It helped me comprehend an important reality: The two-way character of communication between God and the human heart helps us receive the larger gospel.

In addition to that experience blessing my friend, it also blessed me. In the practical undertaking of sharing the gospel in that situation, I came across a fresh way of expressing the gospel with concepts and vocabulary conforming closely to the life and experience of the person to whom I was speaking. To see the validity of the gospel I had known since childhood, taking that new and valid form in a prison encouraged me to seek and practice the principle of restating the Scripture with messages both faithful and creative. In seeking to communicate the gospel in both its original and relevant forms, each of these three factors must be allowed to play its proper role: communication by word, message through actions, and the guidance and power of the Holy Spirit. In this and countless other ways, we can fulfill Jesus' promises regarding the action of the Spirit. We can take what is implicit in the Scriptures and make the truths explicit. Once again, we will experience the Holy Spirit leading us into all truth with all kinds of people.

## Rev. Dr. Cedric Jaggard

Rev. Dr. Cedric Jaggard was born on Thanksgiving Day, November 25, 1915, in Glen Ridge, NJ. He was married to Jean Dale McGiffert Jaggard for 72 years. He is survived by two sons and a daughter, a son - and a daughter-in-law, six grandchildren, and nine great-grandchildren.

Ced received a BA (Greek major) from Dartmouth College when he graduated in 1937. In 1938 He graduated from Haverford College with a Master's Degree in Philosophy. He spent a year of study in Switzerland at the University of Basel in 1938/39, while attending numerous discussions led by Karl Barth, one of the 20th century's most prominent theologians. He was privileged to be under the tutelage of Reinold Niebuhr and Paul Tillich, two other theological giants of the 20th century. Ced continued his education at Union Theological Seminary where he graduated in 1941 with a Master's of Divinity. In 1950, he received his ThD from Princeton Theological Seminary. Cedric served in subsequent pastorates in Valley Stream, NY, Phillipsburg, NJ, Cedar Grove, WI; and Richfield, WI.

He enjoyed teaching theology at Carroll College (now University), and Sociology at the Milwaukee School of Engineering in WI.

Ced served for 23 years as a Chaplain in the Army Reserve.

### Joel E. Kok, Ph.D.

As the child of a military chaplain, Joel attended eight different schools in his K-12 years of education. Following that mixed experience, Joel enjoyed his years of higher learning; he graduated from Calvin University in 1982 (B.A.), Calvin Seminary in 1986 (M. Div.), and Duke University in 1993 (Ph. D.). At Duke, Joel earned his degree under the mentorship of Dr. David Steinmetz. Dr. Steinmetz spoke often of "catholicizing" his students, by which he meant teaching them to **pass on** the universality and fullness of the Christian tradition. Trusting in Christ Jesus as "the way, the truth, and the life" (John 14:6) does not mean acting in an exclusive way that dehumanizes others. Instead, it means uniting with Christ as the Source for a love that **reaches** to all humans and even to all creatures (Ephesians 1:10).